TP on AB

The Life & Times of Tom Powell

Tim O'Brien

Casa Flamingo Literary Arts
Nashville, TN 37221
www.casaflamingo.com

Dedication:

To all the wonderful storytellers out there.

You help make the world a fun, colorful place.

Copyright © 2004 by Tim O'Brien
All rights reserved
Printed and bound in the United States of America

No part of this book may be reproduced or transmitted in any form or by any means, electronic or mechanical, without prior written permission from the publisher. Reviewers may quote brief passages in a review to be printed in a magazine, newspaper, or on the Web, without permission. For information, please contact Tim O'Brien at Casa Flamingo Literary Arts, 6224 Deerbrook Dr., Nashville, Tennessee 37221; www.casaflamingo.com; tim@casaflamingo.com

First printing 2004
ISBN 0-9743324-1-0 - Softcover
ISBN 0 9743324-0-2 - Hardcover
Library of Congress Control Number: 2003111844

Cover illustration: Ken Henley
Cover design: Don Olea
Text & Page design: Tim O'Brien

For additional softcover copies of "TP on AB," or for a collector's limited edition hardcover copy, see ordering information on page 197 of this book, or go to www.casaflamingo.com

Acknowledgements and Sources

So many people helped me in so many ways putting this project together. Below is a list of those who helped, please forgive me if I left your name off. I'll thank you personally.

For taking the time to talk with me about TP, many thanks go to: Albert Carollo, Dennis Carollo, Bob Childress, David Conedara, Tony Conway, Charlie Cox, Frank Curry, Jim Dalrymple, Danny Davis, Donna Dowless, Jimmy Drew, John Friedmann, Carol Fry, Dick Geyer, Bud Gilmore, Dan Glosser, John Graff, Dave Higginbotton, John Hobbs, Robert Johnson, Alieta Klinger, Howard Lander, Tommy Lasorda, Bobby Leonard, Bill Lordy, Bill Luther, Charley Manley, Monsignor Robert J. McCarthy, Wayne McCary, J. Bruce McKinney, George Millay, Stan Minker, Don Mooradian, Max Mosner, Don Muret, Jim Murphy, David Norton, Karen Oertley, Ray Pilszak, Christine Powell, Tom Powell, Bob Reid, Neil Regan, Don Sandefur, Paul Serff, George Smith, Richard Thomas, Thaxter Trafton, Father John Vakulskas, Ray Waddell, and Keith Wright.

The *Amusement Business* archives were quite valuable and I spent hours in the morgue. Thanks to Publisher and Editor-in-Chief Karen Oertley for permission to use them for research and for special permission to use the copyrighted "TP on AB" name.

The oral history project tapes recorded by Bob Reid, and supplied by Dean Justice from the archives of the Society for the Preservation of Professional Touring Entertainment History at the University of Texas, Austin were a big help. Thanks for letting me listen to them.

The (very long) videotape of the TP Appreciation Dinner, held in Denver, provided by Don Sandefur was quite valuable, but a bit boring after awhile.

Father Mac, The Carny Priest, a book about Monsignor Robert J. McCarthy, written by Tom Powell in 1996, provided a good insight into the relationship between those two legends.

The most time-consuming research, but definately the most important and most revealing source of TP info were his nearly 1,000 "TP on AB" columns. I read every word of every column he wrote.

And a Few Kudos

Special thanks to concessionaire Charlie Cox for his behind-the-scenes support and encouragement and his entrepreneur and business advice. I can't begin to say how much help he was with this project.

Thanks to my wife Kathleen, my best friend, for her advice, her proofreading, graphic, and editorial skills, as well as for her support that allowed me to spend hundreds of hours creating this work.

Also, big thanks go out to Kim Bevel who transcribed many, many hours of interviews for me, trying to spell names of unknowns and in dealing with the very colorful and often obnoxious language of the industry.

Table of Contents

Prologue 8
Introduction 9

1- *Who Is Tom Powell?*
Everyone seems to know TP 11

2- *TP Joins AB*
How he got his job and his early days at the publication 13

3- *Welcome To The Rest of Your Life!*
TP goes to his first industry convention 15

4- *The AB Friendship Team*
Working with best friends Howard Lander & Ray Pilszak 17

5- *The AB Doldrums*
How the friendship team saved Amusement Business 21

6- *Life Begins in Bellevue*
TP's early years - from birth through college in Scranton 25

7- *Mr. Powell Goes to Washington*
TP heads to DC as an accountant 29

8- *The Weekly Letter From Home*
"TP on AB" - Excerpts from the column that made him famous .. 33

9- *The Serious Messages*
Using his column to talk about serious issues 43

10- *Meeting, Loving, Losing & Winning Christine*
TP's 11-year courtship of Christine Reid 47

11- *A Series of Super Bowls*
Attending the big games in the name of work 53

12- *TP Meets His Sports Heroes*
Meeting Ted Williams & Stan Musial among others 57

13- *TP Coaches The Globetrotters*
Signing autographs and other stories 63

14- *Even TP Can't Win Them All*
When it comes to betting, don't follow his advice 67

15- *Always Helps To Know The Bar Keep*
Meet TP's best friend, Nashville Palace owner John Hobbs 69

16- *Knowing Minnesota Fats*
TP photographs and plays pool with the legend 71

17- TP Meets The Stars
Becoming friends with Randy Travis and Willie Nelson 73

18- TP & Buddy Lee
Star-studded adventures with the Nashville promoter 79

19- The Airport Connection
TP met the coolest of them all in First Class 83

20- Scotch & Water, Please
Stories of the legendary Scotch drinker 85

21- The Duke in TP's Life
His long friendship with Duke Smith 91

22- The Rabbi in TP's Life
Carnival owner Milt Kaufman always had a story 95

23- TP Meets The Prez
Chatting with President Clinton at the White House 97

24- The Priest in TP's Life
Father Mac befriends the Catholic journalist 99

25- Fun & Travels with Father Mac
TP explores Europe with the Carny Priest 103

26- TP's European Adventures
Getting lost at Oktoberfest and frisked in Milan 107

27- TP's Annual Visit To Scranton
Sharing stories with his hometown buddies 115

28- Kisses & Hugs In Hershey
The Hersheypark red carpet is rolled out when TP visits 119

29- TP Visits The Knoebels
Friends, food & drinks in Elysburg, Pa. 121

30- Living As a Legend
It's not always easy being a legend 123

31- TP the Toastmaster
Not only does he write well, he's a great speaker 125

32- First & Always a Journalist
TP professes love and loyalty for his chosen profession 129

33- Learning The Personal Side
Personal stories from industry leaders 137

34- Hail Fellow, Well Met
TP's friends praise him for his trustworthiness 139

35- Always There For His Friends
Testimonials of how he has remained true to his friends 143

36- How Suite It Is!
   Views from the inside of the IAAM AB Suite 149
37- The Tom Powell Memorial Softball Game
   The games went on until the beer ran out 153
38- TP Gets Roasted
   Bad jokes and good friends were plentiful 157
39- TP's Health Issues: What's Up Doc?
   His battle with a heart attack, hip replacements and cancer 161
40- TP Interviews PT Barnum
   He took this one-on-one talk for granite 167
41- AB Staff Roasts TP
   The staff turns on TP on his 50th birthday 169
42- Carnivals: The Long Love Affair
   His heart is with the showmen 171
43- TP Climbs Onto His Soapbox
   He points out more than a few of his pet peeves 177
44- TP Travels The Fair Circuit
   How fair managers love to wine and dine their favorite editor . . 181
45- The Las Vegas Gathering
   TP visits with the world's top showmen and fairmen 187
46- The Travails of Dr. Tom
   TP misses his plane and his friends plan a scam 189
47- Epilogue: The Beat Goes On
   Tom & Christine - Happily ever after 191

TP and Christine being escorted in style to the dais at the Greater Tampa (Fla.) Showmen's Association banquet.

Prologue

This book chronicles the life and times of Tom Powell, the larger-than-life former editor and now associates publisher of *Amusement Business*, an outdoor amusement industry business-to-business weekly newspaper.

In his 30-plus years with the publication, TP, as he is known to most, has become a celebrity journalist. He has won a bevy of awards during his days, has been officially roasted, and has judged everything from parade floats and fair queens to barbecue and sweet corn.

Amusement Business has a long and colorful history. Founded as *The Billboard* in 1894 in Cincinnati, Ohio, the publication grew along with the live entertainment business. Through the years, it chronicled every industry that "sold fun for profit," including fairs, carnivals, amusement parks, Vaudeville, radio, record companies, television and video. By 1961, it had grown so large and was covering so many different entertainment industries, a decision to divide the coverage was made and *The Billboard* and *Amusement Business* became two separate publications, owned by the same corporation.

The two magazines are still owned by the same parent company, VNU USA, a Dutch company that also owns dozens of additional business-to-business magazines, trade shows, and e-media properties.

Old timers in the carnival, fair and amusement park industries still call *Amusement Business* the *Billboard* and it is still considered by most as the Bible of the outdoor amusement industry.

TP arrived in 1972 at a time the newspaper and the industries it served needed a strong personality, a celebrity journalist that could pull it all together. TP soon filled those shoes and became a legend in the process.

Introduction

If it weren't for Tom Powell, I wouldn't have my career at *Amusement Business*. I interviewed with him back in mid-1985, he liked me and hired me as his managing editor.

This is a story that needed to be told. It's a work of love and admiration. I was impressed with his old time journalism style. He drank Scotch, but (as far as I know) never kept a bottle in his desk drawer as the movie-style journalists always did. He wears glasses, but I never saw him with a green visor shade.

He was already a legend of sorts when I met him. The newspaper was popular, advertising sales were good, and we all traveled a great deal.

I've written nearly a dozen books and literally thousands of articles through the years. During that time, I've learned to spot a good story when I see one.

After working with TP for 18 years, I decided his story was ready to be told. Maybe he's not as interesting as a movie star, and maybe he's not as articulate as a politician, but TP doesn't take a back seat to anyone when it comes to telling a great story or working a room.

Tom and I have become great working friends and he was best man at

Country music stars Wynonna and Naomi Judd visit with TP.

my wedding in 1996. I have him on videotape singing to my bride, Kathleen. He toasted us with a wonderful Irish toast he borrowed from the late and great Irishman and amusement park pioneer, Ken Wynne. Tom is a practicing Catholic and for years I jokingly addressed him each morning as Pope Tom. He was never discouraged by that repartee.

He has always been there for me to talk with, and he has remained loyal, not only to me but to his myriad friends, his family, and surprisingly, the magazine itself. Badmouth *Amusement Business* in front of Tom, and you'll surely get a quick and strong response.

TP, circa 1980

Tommy Lasorda, the Los Angeles Dodgers manager and Baseball Hall of Fame member, a long time friend of Tom Powell gave me a pep talk as I was gathering information for the book. "Tom is a great man, a wonderful man. You have to write this book so that the people who read it know what a great man he really is," he instructed me. "It should be a best seller," he added. I guess he always thinks big!

The story as it unfolds here is not your basic biography. Most of the words come from people who know Tom. It's certainly a biased biography. I didn't try to dig up any dirt. I didn't talk with the two or three people out there that don't like him, and I didn't write everything I know about him. I also didn't have space to write all the stories related to me by his friends or to write of all his travels, adventures and experiences. I'm saving those for the sequel.

In places, this book will not read like a published biography, but more like a collection of stories and tributes. I didn't follow the "proper" writing methods. Instead I wrote to communicate a fun story. A fun and often heartfelt story of a great Irishman who is cool enough to be able to call several sideshow freaks, sports heroes, and stars of the stage and screen as his friends.

Tim O'Brien
Nashville, Fall 2003

1

WHO IS TOM POWELL?

Brenda and Eddie are in Rome, standing outside the Vatican. Two men come out on the veranda. One is wearing a robe, a tall hat and is blessing everyone. The other fellow is a rotund, gray haired man wearing glasses, suspenders and waving to everyone.

Eddie to Brenda: Who is that?

Brenda: I don't know who the guy is with the hat, but the other guy is Tom Powell.

An old joke - but probably not far from the truth.

But Really, Who is Tom Powell?

Thomas Joseph Powell was born in Bellevue, a middle-class Irish section of Scranton, Pa. His father was a coal miner, his mother a housewife.

He was a normal child. His best friend growing up claims that Tom was "kind of dorky."

Tom wanted to be a baseball player.

Tom wanted to be a sports writer.

Tom wanted to meet Ted Williams.

Tom wanted to coach the Harlem Globetrotters.

More than 70 years later, Tom has done all that, but what he really has excelled at is being TOM POWELL, Mr. *Amusement Business*, a true legend in his own time.

Well, really a legend in his spare time, because of all the journalists who have written a story, it's hard to believe that any could be more prolific than TP,

Tim on TP

I found writing this book a real challenge. I hate redundancy, but by the third chapter I ran out of ways of saying drunk, drinking, etc.

- Tim O'Brien

National Ticket Company's Bill Alter, baseball great Joe DiMaggio, and TP.

as he has been called since his first column ran at AB in 1979.

To many, TP is the face of AB. His column, "TP on AB" dropped names of just about everyone working in the live entertainment industry during the 20-some years it ran. Tom has written more articles on the carnival, arena, park and fair industries than anyone else in the world.

His memory of the details, his ability to recall a person's name after meeting them once, and his caring conversations with everyone from the top music stars and politicians to the carnival sideshow men are legendary.

It seems just about everyone knows Tom Powell. If you don't, here's an opportunity to get to know the guy simply known as TP.

2

TP JOINS AB

Discreetly tucked away on Page 9 of the July 15, 1972 edition of *Amusement Business*, a 31-line announcement was the first most readers ever heard of Tom Powell:

"Tom Powell, veteran writer in the sports and auditorium and arena fields has joined the editorial staff of *Amusement Business*. He will attend the San Diego conference of International Association of Auditorium Managers (as his first assignment). Powell, 39, is a native of Scranton, Pa., who worked in the news department of the *Scrantonian-Tribune*, and spent 15 years in the sports department of Nashville's *The Tennessean*. He was editor for one year of the International Rodeo Assn.'s publication, *Rodeo News*. During that time he was in charge of all IRA public relations. He specialized in automobile racing but also covered major sports events such as championship fights, football bowl games, hockey, basketball, and personality features. He is a graduate of the University of Scranton."

That was it. Welcome to the rest of your life. Little could he realize what was in store for him.

Tom came to Middle Tennessee originally in 1956 when he was stationed at Fort Campbell Army base in Clarksville for two years. By the time he was discharged in 1958, he had married a Nashville girl and had started a family. He got a job at the daily newspaper in Nashville, *The Tennessean*, as a sports writer. After 15 years at the daily, he felt he needed a change, left Music City and took a job back in Scranton at the *Scrantonian-Tribune* where his journalistic career started several decades earlier.

"My marriage was in trouble and I thought if I moved back to Scranton it might salvage it," Tom recalls. He moved in with his father, expecting his family to join him once he bought a house. However, he only stayed in Scranton for three months.

Tom had met Walt Heeney, then publisher of *Amusement Business* in the late 1960s when he was doing some work with the locally-based Longhorn Rodeo, owned by Bruce Lehrke. In fact, while Tom was International Rodeo

Association (IRA) Publicity Director, his first by-line appeared in AB. It was a column that ran February 14, 1970 about the importance of the rodeo as a sport and how important the IRA was to the sport.

Following that article, Walt Heeney offered him a job but Tom didn't take it. Following that short stint in Scranton and after he realized he wanted to be in Nashville, TP gave Heeney a call. "I said if you want me half as much as you did two years ago I want you twice as bad now, so he offered me $1,000 less than he had offered before knowing I was anxious to come back."

A young TP gets instructions from city editor Herman Eskew during his early days at The Tennessean newspaper in Nashville.

TP and Heeney made plans to finalize the employment deal during Heeney's upcoming trip to New York City. TP took a bus from Scranton, wearing his finest suit of clothes. "I tried to look my best."

From the Port Authority Bus Station he walked to a hotel to meet Heeney. It was raining, he had no umbrella, and TP and his new suit got drenched. "I looked like hell I'm sure. We met, and he said lets go have a beer and everything good happened over the next three to six beers. He officially hired me and said he was going to put me in charge of AB's new division covering ice rinks."

One question remained in the interview.

"He asked me if I knew anything about ice rinks. I said, oh, sure, which, of course I didn't. And the one sport I never really cared much about was hockey but I wanted the job so I said, yeah, I can cover ice rinks."

TP went back to Scranton, gathered up his belongings, and moved back to Nashville to start a new life. He rented an apartment, officially separated from his wife and went to work for *Amusement Business* as a reporter.

3

WELCOME TO THE REST OF YOUR LIFE

Tom Powell walked through the front door of AB's Nashville office in mid-June, met a few fellow workers, picked up his note pad and became part of the arena coverage team. Heeney's idea of expanding ice rink coverage never got anywhere.

Lucky for TP.

The 1972 convention of the International Association of Auditorium Managers (IAAM) in San Diego in late July was TP's first of the thousands of road trips he would eventually travel for *Amusement Business*.

Heeney, along with editor Irwin Kirby and TP represented the editorial side of AB at that convention and right from the beginning, TP showed he was a prolific writer with a good memory.

"I've never had a more satisfying convention than that one because when I left to come home I had no notes. Every time I covered a session I'd go to a room and write it up. I came back to Nashville with nothing to write and more than 20 finished stories."

However, TP's first of many run-ins with Kirby came at that point.

Editor Kirby said he didn't want reporters to send any stories until he checked them first, and realizing that would slow the process down, TP went to Heeney, explained the situation and Heeney told him to go ahead and send them.

From then on Kirby and Heeney "were always at each other's throat and I was always in the middle. Irwin was always badmouthing Walt. Walt never badmouthed him, but he took it. He knew Irwin was badmouthing him. And I just listened."

Bob Kendall, who was then associate publisher gave TP a bit of advice back then. "Just keep your mouth shut; don't say anything; keep your nose clean." It's a lesson to which TP still adheres to this day.

The Journey

An editorial shakeup began in August 1974 when Heeney named TP managing editor and gave him complete responsibility for the news content of the magazine. Editor Kirby was moved into the associate publisher's post where he headed up the new Editorial Projects Department overseeing AB's special issues and directories.

In reality, Kirby was out of the way, and TP stepped into a position of power for the first time. "I had never worked in anything other than a seniority system and I never dreamed I'd get anywhere here until somebody died and here he put me over a guy who'd been editor for 23 years."

In retrospect, putting TP in charge was probably one of the smartest things Heeney did during his tenure at AB. It began a new era, one that proved to be one of the most profitable in the newspaper's history.

TP became AB's official editorial leader in May 1975. He had been with the newspaper for nearly three years by then and had been building his power base. Now, he was free to start becoming legendary.

It didn't take him long to warm up to the industries, to realize that he had something special here to write about. While always a skilled and professional journalist, TP soon became an important part of the community in which he chronicled.

He quickly made friends in both high and low places. Many of the friends he met during those first several years of working at AB are still his buddies.

"Sure, I have met a lot of people while going after a story, but I never befriended someone just to get close to them in order to get a story. I value friendships too much for that kind of stuff."

Concessionaire Charlie Cox and TP at the White House.

4

THE AB FRIENDSHIP TEAM

As TP was making friends with the industry, friendships also blossomed among colleagues at AB. For nearly two decades, the team of Tom Powell, Howard Lander and Ray Pilszak was the face of AB to the public. Sure there were others, but these three seemed inseparable. It was good chemistry, at least for awhile.

Lander and TP were given the name of Fric and Frac by then associate publisher Bob Kendall. Someone else nicknamed TP and Pilszak the odd couple. Both were quite appropriate monikers.

The 22-year old Lander joined AB in 1975 as a reporter, entering the scene when AB was struggling a bit and during a time when discord was prevalent within the ranks. "There was no sense of team work at that time," Lander recalls.

He remembers one of his first editorial meetings in publisher Heeney's office, before TP became editor.

"Irwin (Kirby, the editor) didn't like Tom because he was threatened by him. We're sitting around in Heeney's office preparing to go to the 1975 park convention. Irwin was giving out all the assignments and he didn't want to give any to Tom. I'm on the job a month and they're loading me up and they're not giving him anything. I'm thinking a lot of things, but I'm not saying anything."

Tom wasn't mad at Lander, but he did comment to Heeney about giving all the good stories to the punk kid and not getting any for himself.

In those days the staff drove everywhere they could with usually three or four to a car. The parks' convention was to be in Atlanta, an easy four-hour drive from Nashville, so TP said he would drive on that occasion.

Lander and TP were set to share a room.

"Kirby could make a person nervous as could be and he was making my life miserable on this trip. Tom took me under his wing, told me not to worry about things and said he would edit my stories before I sent them back," Lander said.

The two had a good time and their friendship got off to a good start. They were both single, they both liked to drink and they both, as former sports writers had a lot to talk about. The close friendship lasted nearly 15 years until Lander moved up the corporate ladder to New York.

At first, Lander and TP worked together as reporters. Then TP became editor and Howard worked for him. In 1976, Lander moved to the NYC office and switched to advertising sales, which meant he then worked for Ray Pilszak. He was promoted to publisher in 1980 and moved back to Nashville in 1981.

> **TP ON TP**
>
> "Ray Pilszak, our aging salesman, always kidded that he worked hard selling space in AB and I had no problem giving it away."
>
> -Tom Powell

Funtimes As A Trio

Lander said everything he did with TP in those days was fun. "We'd be watching a football game or going to a convention, or driving to Tampa for 14 hours. They were just wonderful, wonderful times. Most of the time, I couldn't stop laughing."

TP and Pilszak quickly became the odd couple and they bickered all the time, Lander said.

"I would egg them on. One time we're at Tom's apartment and we're playing a card game, Tonk. To make a long story short Tom accuses us of changing the rules and he refused to play. We had come over to play and watch TV. There was a game on and we were going to have some pizza. He was furious with us."

Tonk is a game you can play with 2, 3, 4 people so when TP quit Pilszak and Lander kept playing. "Tom was sitting there seething and you could see he wanted to throw us out but he couldn't because he invited us over. So I finally said aren't you going to order the pizza? He was so angry with us. He was furious."

Today, Pilszak says the bickering between the two wasn't all that serious. "No, it was usually nothing personal, I just liked to tear into him just to get his dander up. He loves to dish it out but he hates to take it."

In 1973, in what he calls "a terrible mistake and something that he is ashamed of," TP got married again, a union that lasted for a short period. His friends stood by him during that period, and Lander and TP ended up living together for eight months after TP's divorce. They were both single and TP who was Lander's boss at the time, insisted the two live together for a short time while he got back on his feet.

As editor, TP was always expected to attend the sales meetings and talk about editorial with the sales staff. One of the meetings was held near Nashville at Montgomery Bell State Park where staff members stayed in rustic cabins.

Salesmen Pilszak and Lander were slated to be roommates and when TP came out for his presentation, plans were for the three to hang out after the meetings, play cards and have a few drinks. They insisted that TP spend the night with them and head back to the office the following morning.

Around 3 a.m. they decided to conclude the poker game and go to bed. Since Tom was only going to be there one night, he was to sleep on a fold-up rollaway bed.

After retiring, Tom started playing around and kept reaching over and pulling Pilszak's blankets off the bed. Pilszak kept telling him to stop it because he wanted to get to sleep. Tom didn't stop. Pilszak lost his patience, jumped off the bed, grabbed Tom, shoved him sideways in the bed and folded him up and locked him in. Tom's feet were hanging out one end and his head was hanging out the other, locked in. Pilszak is quick to point out that TP was "much thinner in those days, making it possible for me to latch the bed shut. I could never do that to him today."

> ### POWER WHAT???
>
> "One day Tom decided that he wanted a new car and dragged me along to the dealer where he saw a good looking blue Ford. He looked it over and told the dealer that he would take it. I said, Tom, aren't you going to drive it? He said, 'no, it will be OK, it's a new car.' Tom bought it and about a week later he tells me how hard it is to steer. I asked if he had power steering and he didn't know for sure, but it turns out he didn't. He tried to take it back but the dealer said he was sorry but he couldn't take it back because it was a used car."
>
> — Ray Pilszak

Who's The Boss?

Lander left the team in 1976 to work in sales for another publication in *The Billboard* family in New York, but he rejoined AB as a salesman a few years later and was soon made publisher.

When Lander moved back to Nashville as top dog in 1981, it added an entirely new dynamic to the office. Lander had worked for Tom as a reporter, and he had worked for Pilszak in sales in New York. He came back and was the boss to them both.

Lander recalls how Pilszak and TP both took immediate advantage of the new relationship.

"We go out to lunch the first day and you know here's my editor and my sales director. So I buy them lunch. The second day we're at another restaurant and they don't make a move for their wallets so I buy them lunch again. Now the third day the check comes and again they don't move. I said if you guys think I'm buying you lunch every day this is the last lunch we're ever going to have together. So, of course, they just figured as long as I was willing to pick it up they were going to let me do it."

Lander said it wasn't as awkward as it might seem to come back as the boss of two people who had helped train him and had become good buddies in the process.

"It really wasn't because we were friends. When I worked for those guys it wasn't really a boss-employee relationship. So when the shoe was on the other foot nothing really changed for a long time," Lander said.

AB's three amigos Ray Pilszak, Howard Lander and Tom Powell, with Roger Staubach, seated at left, and Terry Bradshaw.

5

THE AB DOLDRUMS

Howard Lander returned to AB with the attitude that there was only one way for the newspaper to go and that was up. He felt it needed a fresh makeover, a new design, better paper stock, a concentrated effort to get arenas to advertise, and a rededication to the industries it had been covering for decades.

TP, Ray Pilszak and Lander worked together to successfully make those changes and by mid-1980s, AB was back on top.

During this period, the three still hung together both at work and at play. "I remember one time I took a week off and I wasn't going out of town," Lander said. "I just took time off and Gail, my wife, said you know you can't be doing business. At that time I had young kids and I promised that I wouldn't work and we could do day trips and that sort of stuff."

Several days into the vacation, Lander, the kids and Gail went to lunch at a popular family-oriented restaurant. They go in, sit down and it wasn't long before Gail noticed that TP and Pilszak were having lunch at a nearby table. She invited them to come over and join the Lander clan.

Was it a coincidence or was it planned? "Of course it was all planned, those guys would never eat lunch at a place like that on their own."

Non-Corporate Environment

A much different company owned *Amusement Business* at that time. It was privately held up through the 80s and employees felt a strong bond to the company.

"I mean we'd be in the office on Christmas Day. I'd be there and all of a sudden I'd hear Ray whistling and then later Tom would come in," said Lander. "AB was just different and I think the three of us were the right people at the right time. I'm not sure we could do it now. I'm not sure the personal relationships would make that kind of difference."

Pilszak recalls those times as "a hell of a lot of fun," and agrees with Lander that it probably couldn't happen again in these days of corporate mentality. "When AB and (its sister publication) Billboard were owned by the Littleford family, it was a family operation and we wanted to work our

TP interviews and plays around with 1932 Heavyweight Champion, Jack Sharkey.

ass off for them, but it was a fun time too. People appreciated the effort and the loyalty more then than they do now," Pilszak said.

Under Lander's vision, the three worked hard to create an identity for AB during those years. "We covered the live entertainment industry, and we spent a lot of time going to functions, events, and other activities that were part of our coverage, and that really helped us build the publication into a strong one. It was hard work and took a lot of time, but it really was worth it, for us personally and for the newspaper," Pilszak said. "It looked glamorous to our readers, but it was very hard work and required a strong devotion to what we were doing."

To this day, Howard, who has made a name for himself and is one of the top leaders of VNU Inc., which owns both AB and Billboard, says those days in the 70s and 80s with TP and Pilszak were "some of the happiest years I've had during my career."

Good To Be Friends

Lander felt it was quite appropriate for the three to be best friends. He said the newspaper actually worked better because of that friendship. TP, the editor dominated the attention the publication was getting. Lander often said, even when he was publisher, that people thought he was along just to carry TP's luggage.

"No one gave a shit who I was. First of all, I was much younger. They couldn't get it that I was the publisher. When I took over I said Tom, you can do whatever you want. You just have to let me point you in the direction. Let me set the agenda. You and Ray can be out front. I don't care. I just want to make money and that's exactly what it was about."

TP, Howard Lander and Ray Pilszak brought AB back from the doldrums in the early 1980s.

Lander believed the editor was the most important person on the publication, more so than even the publisher. "If you have the right kind of editor, which we did, he sold the publication."

Karen Oertley was promotions manager during that period and was promoted to the publisher's chair in 1990. She recalls working with the three amigos in those days.

"They certainly brought an energy to the publication and there was an energy going on at the same time in the business and the forces united and it was a great time for a lot of us at *Amusement Business*," Oertley said. "They were a good team. They had a lot of fun together. They were good friends."

When Lander left for New York in 1988 to work at the corporate level, his close relationship with TP became a bit tenuous and began to fade. Lander had other duties in New York, but was still responsible for *Amusement Business*. "The industry was changing. The demands on the publication were growing. My role had changed and it became a bit of a strain at times when you have to be able

Ray Pilszak and TP, known to many as The Odd Couple.

to separate the friendships from the business obligations and responsibilities that I had," Lander said.

Oertley first became general manager and eventually took over as publisher after Lander went to New York and as a result, became TP's boss. Then in 1994, when TP became associate publisher, a promotion that he saw as a demotion, she became editor-in-chief.

At that point in his career, many felt TP was doomed, but he remained a gentleman and a professional and persevered through an obviously stressful transition and hurtful time in his life. Oertley recalls the time as a positive challenge for both of them.

"A lot of people didn't think I could be successful because Tom has a very strong, well-known personality. He's strong. He's a big, tall man with a big, loud voice. Many people in the industry thought it was going to be a lot tougher time than it actually was for Tom and I. People in the industry have gotten to know me better and now understand what the business needs were at the time and why the changes were made. You know they've come to realize that it wasn't such a disaster for Tom or his career."

While Tom was upset and felt he had been derailed, he loved the publication, the industry, and his industry friends too much to make a big deal out of it publicly. He adapted to his new role and wrote more stories than he ever had. But he says the hurt and the feeling of betrayal will always be with him.

Racecar driver and country music crooner Marty Robbins, with TP and an unidentified assistant.

6

LIFE BEGINS IN BELLEVUE

President Franklin D. Roosevelt was a busy man and probably wasn't aware that Alice and Tom Powell of Bellevue, Pa., a section of Scranton, gave birth to their first child, a son on the night of July 18, 1933.

Coincidentally, the birth took place only a few days after the first-ever major league all-star baseball game was played. Tom grew up to be a non-political huge baseball fan.

His father went to school until the fifth grade before he dropped out and went to work in the mines in Taylor, Pa., for the Moffit Coal Company. His mother, as well as most other members in the neighborhood were housewives and didn't work outside the home.

Tom was five years old when his brother Bob was born. The two shared the early days together and shared a deep love of family, the neighborhood and each other, but had different interests. For example, TP lived for sports and wanted to talk about them all the time. Bob didn't like sports quite as much. Though distance separated them for their entire adult life, Tom felt solace in the fact they were still always there for each other.

Tom Recalls His Early Years

"It was a great home life. I grew up in a neighborhood of mostly Irish Catholics. My father was the second Protestant and the second Republican in the Bellevue neighborhood, a four-block area. He was kind of an individualist, and I have often thought I wish I were more like him.

"My father never did convert. My brother, mother, and I were all Catholics, but everybody on my father's side were Protestant. Ironically when my mother died it was the Protestants who really looked after us, cooked meals for us, ironed our clothes, and did everything for us."

Tom's mother died at the age of 53 from cancer. "I was a sophomore in college and one of the biggest regrets of my life was that she wasn't there when I graduated. The only reason I went to college was because she pushed me into it."

His father lived until he was 72. He died of diabetes but was also suffering from black lung disease. His brother Bob died of cancer in 1997 at the age of 58.

Despite the hard work and the knowledge of black lung, Tom wanted to work in the mines during the summer because of the "big money" the coal companies were paying.

However, his father had other ideas. "He gave me a kick in the rear and said I'd never go down in the mines as long as he was alive."

Tom went to kindergarten through seventh grade in his neighborhood at the Horace Mann School. He then "went up the hill" out of the neighborhood about a mile to West Scranton Senior High School from which he graduated.

Beginning of Sports Fan Tom

Tom says he became a sports nut, in part, because of his father. "My dad and I were both Boston Red Sox fans, mostly Ted Williams fans."

His first non-classroom writing "assignment" was while he was in seventh grade. "I was chosen to write an essay for the Daughters of the American Revolution. I didn't win the contest, but I was the one from my class chosen to write it and that itself seemed like an honor.

Ironically, the two major loves in Tom's life, sports and journalism both began as a result of each other.

He was good at back yard sports and felt he had a good shot at making the school basketball team. He tried out and felt he should have made the team. He didn't and was quite bitter until he found that his father had told the coach not to put him on the team because of TP's heart murmur.

"The heart murmur has never affected me in any way and I got upset with my dad but I knew he thought he was doing the right thing so I got over that."

He got his first "real" newspaper job while a sophomore in high school. He peddled the afternoon paper to about 100 regular customers. Some of that ink must have gotten into his blood.

Since sports were not an option in the ninth grade, Tom decided he wanted to be a sports writer. Not a journalist, but a sports writer. He made friends with the sports editors at Scranton's morning paper and they let him cover a few of the high school games. "They used to kid me and say, do you want a buck or a byline knowing I would take the byline. Seeing 'By Tom Powell' in print meant more to me than anything."

Today, with literally thousands "By Tom Powell" by-lines out there, he laughs at those early days. "I'd probably take the buck today."

College Bound

Although he thought he would like to go to college, Tom didn't think he would ever be able to afford tuition. Both his parents insisted that he go.

"Here I am sweeping floors in a factory where foul-mouthed women are cursing and calling me everything underneath the sun and I'm getting paid 75-cents an hour. Three days before college starts and my mother and father said you're going to college.

"I said, no, I'm not; you can't afford to send me, and they said we'll pay the first semester and you'll have to work for the rest. It was $261.50 a semester and we really couldn't afford it, but they came up with the money and I worked at least for 40 hours a week for the next four years to pay my way through college. I wouldn't recommend it to anybody, but it was the only way I could have gotten through."

He went to the University of Scranton, a Jesuit, Catholic school. He lived at home and walked 23 minutes to school everyday. The school didn't

Notre Dame football coach Lou Holtz and T.P.

offer journalism, his first choice, so he settled on accounting and graduated in four years.

His first real job with a newspaper was in college. Jimmy Calpin was the assistant sports editor of the Scranton Tribune and he got Tom a job as a copy boy from 10 p.m. to midnight at 75-cents an hour. Then he worked his way through the other copy boy slots and worked in the morgue (library) filing photos. He recalls that the sports department liked him.

"All the sports writers took me under their wing and when they'd have their opening day predictions of who was going to win the pennant, they included me and I got to cover some of the games."

In 1955, with little spare time on his hands because of his work and school schedules, he found time to organize an intramural softball team. He recruited, he managed, and he pitched the team to the intramural championship for the University of Scranton.

"By that time my father had retired from the coal mines and had a

Elvis Presley's manager Col. Tom Parker and TP.

political job at Clark's Summit Hospital through the Republicans. My mother was dead, so when I came home there was nobody there; nobody to tell me what to do or put a leash on me.

"Many nights when I'd walk home from school or work, maybe at 1 or 2 a.m., I'd go by Bonadio's Bar, which was right across the street from where I lived. There I'd see my friends; Tom Connolly, Chappy Fanning, Jack O'Connor, and some other guys, and I'd join them.

"At that time I wasn't drinking. Believe it or not, I was drinking Pepsi and eating pizzas and eating pretzels and stuff like that. I can't tell you how many nights I walked out of there at 7 or 8 in the morning and walked to school without having gone home.

7

MR. POWELL GOES TO WASHINGTON

Upon graduation from college, Tom left Bellevue and went out into the world for the very first time, completely on his own.

He went to work with the General Accounting Office in Washington, D.C. He started out with a GS5 ranking and after a couple of months became a GS7. He started out at $3,670 a year and went to $5,470.

He thought he had it made. Good money, a college degree and he was out on his own for the first time in his life, living the furthest from home he had ever been. Five others that he had graduated with joined him in Washington and they became roommates, each paying $32.50 a month in rent for the top floor of a big house located across the street from the Swiss Legation.

No-Money Laundering

To save money on laundry, the guys would drive 240 miles back to their homes in Scranton every weekend.

A year later, on June 23, Uncle Sam came knocking and less than a week later, TP headed back to Scranton to say his good byes to family and friends.

"I had thought by then that the Army surely had forgotten me. I was 23 years old when I got drafted, and they took me in on July 3, 1956. I had planned a big party on the Fourth and they took me in. To this day I'm bitter about going in the army on July 3rd. They could have waited a few days."

Following basic training at Fort Dix, N.J., he was assigned to Fort Campbell, Kentucky, just 55 miles north of Nashville in Clarksville, Tenn., where he would spend his entire length of service.

He worked in the finance office. While there, he met his first wife, Rosamond Mattimore, who mothered his four children, Julia, Alice, Tommy, and Kevin.

Army life was good for Tom and his young family. "Once we got married and lived off post it was a breeze. I was working with civilians. It was just like a civilian job working 9 to 5."

TP said he was "a lousy soldier and could never figure out how to put my M-1 rifle together," which of course is no surprise to anyone who knows him. He is the first one to admit how "mechanically inept" he is.

One of TP's first columns for The Tennessean.

Being drafted he only had a two-year stint to serve. He wasted no time getting out when he could in July 1958.

Out Of The Army

Knowing that his wife had family in the Nashville area and that she preferred to stay there, Tom checked out *The Tennessean*, the morning daily newspaper in Nashville, hoping to get a job in the sports department.

They hired the 25-year old on the spot for $80 a week. At first, he filed

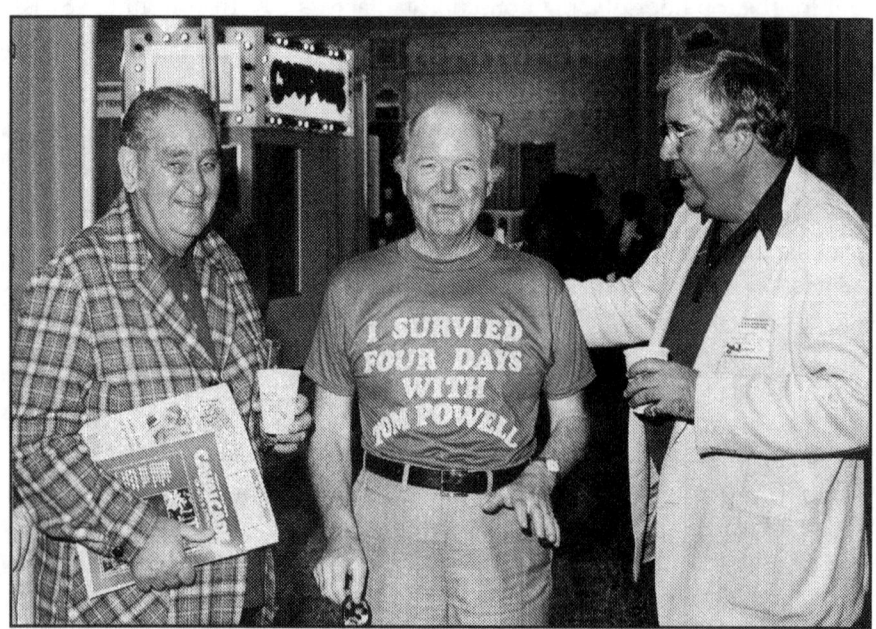

Fort Wayne's Don Myers, center, stayed with TP for four days in Nashville and showed up at the next convention wearing this custom shirt. Notice that he misspelled survived. At left is Bob Barnet, then secretary of the Indiana Association of County and District Fairs.

photos and took game reports on the phone. He learned to work fast and accurately taking football, basketball, track meets, anything that people would call in.

His career at *The Tennessean* was long, from 1958 to 1972. He created his own niches, based both on his personal interests and the needs of the newspaper, just as he did later at *Amusement Business*.

He was assigned to cover local auto racing and every Saturday night he could be found at the Nashville Speedway, not only covering his beat, but making $25 extra a night by serving as the track announcer. He did that for 10 years.

It was during this time that he worked four jobs, not counting his Saturday night announcing gig, to make ends meet. They all fitted him and he says he loved doing it all but the jobs did pull him away from his family a great deal of time.

He was working full-time at *The Tennessean* and part time for WENO Radio where he used the UPI wire service to create six five minute radio shows a day. "The guy kept telling me to do more because he could sell it, and I kept telling him that I had a full-time job and couldn't do anymore. I'd do them in the morning, and mid-afternoon, and at night."

He was also editor of the *Springfield Herald*. Springfield is a town about 40 miles from Nashville and he would go up there Monday and Tuesday "before work" and put out their weekly paper for $75 per week.

In addition, he was editor of Bruce Lehrke's *Rodeo News*, which he did for a couple of years. He said he knew less about rodeos than he did about auto racing, but he learned quickly.

TP visits with basketball great John Havlicek, left, and baseball great Joe DiMaggio.

Surprisingly there was no conflict between all those jobs. "I mostly worked *The Tennessean* from 4 p.m. to 1 a.m. I went to Springfield during the day two days a week. I had a microphone on my desk for WENO Radio and I would spend one Saturday a month putting out the *Rodeo News*."

By January 1972, his life started changing. That's when he left *The Tennessean*, went back to Scranton for three months, got his reporting job with AB and moved back to Nashville. He was back in Music City USA for good by June.

Unknowingly it was then that he began the journey of becoming the best known, the most trusted, and most read journalist to ever cover the outdoor amusement industries.

A legend was born.

Christine and Tom entertain guests in their special corner at their favorite bar, The Nashville Palace.

8

"TP on AB"
THE WEEKLY LETTER FROM HOME

To AB readers, Tom Powell officially became TP for the first time on June 2, 1979 when the first "TP on AB" column appeared. The birth of his column was when his official status as a legend began. Sure, he was already known to many in the industry, but it was through the writings in his "TP on AB" column that his exploits and his personality became known to everyone.

The weekly column, best described as a heart-felt, tell-all letter from home, added a much-needed personal touch to AB coverage and it helped give the newspaper a new personality. When it began, it was the only column in the paper and to most of the readers, it was the only official voice coming from AB. "TP on AB" was many things rolled into one.

It was a gossip column, it was a church bulletin and it was a blow-by-blow account of TP's phone calls, travels and bowling scores. It was the ongoing saga of "aging sales manager" Ray Pilszak and "the weak-eyed publisher" Howard Lander and sometimes it read more like a television sitcom than it did a newspaper column.

Through his column, TP was able to have fun writing and at the same time be as glib as he wanted. On the regular pages of the paper, he had to be an objective journalist. Here, he could be a friend and could voice his personal thoughts while bringing the various areas of AB coverage together as one big family.

> **Tim on TP**
>
> "Even when TP was on the road, long before laptops, he would call in and dictate his column. He would have an idea of what he wanted to say but would just make it up as he went and we would stop him when we felt he had enough to fill his space. It usually turned into a long and arduous task for the reporter, usually right on deadline."
>
> - Tim O'Brien

Each week, he made it a point to include something about each of AB's target markets.

While traveling, before laptops and emails, he would organize a few notes and call the office from his hotel room and dictate the column to whatever reporter was available. His datelines read like a travelogue. One week from Munich; the next from San Francisco.

A Legend is Born

His first column began:

"It seems appropriate that my first column for *Amusement Business* comes almost seven years after I joined Billboard Publications as an AB reporter. The statute of limitations, it would seem, has run out on my apprenticeship."

It didn't take long for him to start the tradition of dropping names. By the time the third paragraph had been written, the likes of Ted Williams, Joe DiMaggio and Cassius Clay had already been mentioned.

Benny "Boom Boom" Koske, the Human Bomb was the first industry name to appear. He was followed in the list by Omar the Snake Man. Buddy Lee, the wrestler who turned promoter extraordinaire was the first talent industry person to be listed and carnival owner Rod Link was the first of the thousand carnies TP would mention during the 22 years the column ran.

The colorful Buddy Clewis, who TP described as the "controversial and outspoken" manager of the Mobile (Ala.) Municipal Auditorium earned the title as being the first facility manager to earn space in the column.

Of all the musical entertainers TP would write about, including the Rolling Stones and Elvis, country crooner Faron Young was the first. TP pointed out it was Young that likened life on the road of an entertainer to the sometimes lonely, nomadic carnival people who take their rides to people in all corners of the world.

Cork Teachworth, then manager of the State Fair of Virginia was the first fair person and Eddie Carroll Sr., owner of Riverside Park (now Six Flags New England) in Agawam, Mass., was the first park owner to hit the column. Other names in that inaugural column included Vince Pantuso of Volume Services, sideshow owners Ward Hall and Chris Christ, and Bill Cunningham, head of the Oakland-Alameda (Calif.) County Coliseum.

One point became clear very fast. AB readers liked reading about their peers and it was TP's generous name-dropping that kept people turning to his column every week.

"Who doesn't like to see their name in print? He wasn't doing it for himself, you know, he was doing it for them. He knew what it meant to them to have their names in print where all their peers would see it," TP's wife Christine points out.

> ### CAN'T FIX IT
>
> *I don't think Tom ever got in the habit of doing things around the house or fixing or building things and that's why he's so mechanically challenged. I think if he had a problem with a toilet at home he'd probably forget about fixing it and go use a public restroom somewhere."*
>
> *- Ray Pilszak*

Schooners of Beer. Great Start!!!

His first reference to his love for the drink came at the end of that first column:

"History records that AB was founded over two schooners of beer in a Kentucky tavern by a couple billposters named Donaldson back in 1894. I'll drink to their dream of serving the entertainment industry. I'll drink to the continued prosperity of our market and friends. And If I can still click the typewriter keys after all those drinks, I'll hoist one more to writing for and about all you interesting people in the weeks, months and years ahead. That's a dream worth fulfilling."

In the third column, Don Myers, a facility manager in Fort Wayne, Ind., made his first appearance in "TP on AB." "Under separate cover, I am forwarding a copy of a column I have written concerning some things I have learned while attending many conventions." Entitled "DM on TP for AB," the column was blank. Through the years, Myers humor and creativity landed him in the column many times.

In addition to using his column to tell the world of his own travels and exploits, he captured the essence of the people in the industry by relaying their phone calls, their messages, their conversations. His column was THE place to have your name mentioned.

He never tried to cover up his intent to name drop. In fact, he was rather proud of getting as many names in the newspaper that he did, and he happily reported the findings of industry veteran Bob Reid who kept score on how many times each name of those in the public facility side were printed.

"I read the column religiously and I began to notice that there seemed to be maybe a dozen people that seemed to get mentioned a little more than the rest of us in the business," Reid said.

In 1988, Reid wrote TP mentioning that "I've noticed that you've mentioned John, Sam, George, Pete, and only occasionally Alice but you seem to mention them a lot compared to other people."

Then Reid got the idea to write down the names as they appeared and send TP a recap at the end of the year. "As I think about this now I probably didn't forewarn him. I probably just decided to do this for one year and I did it religiously. I didn't tell anybody. I had to read every word and then I had to make sure I had the right math and all."

For the next seven years, Reid counted and TP reported the findings. Jim Dalrymple of the D.C. Armory and Robert F. Kennedy Stadium in Washington, D.C. was mentioned the most, with three yearly crowns and Cliff Wallace of Leisure Management landed that distinction twice.

> ## DEFINING TP
>
> *"Tom has easily crossed all the lines in every product that Amusement Business covers. That's why he is Mr. Amusement Business. He feels very comfortable with the carnivals, with the parks, with the arenas, with any aspect of Amusement Business's coverage. He was there and he did more than what was needed. He created the job, the aura, and he stuck with it. He knows how to react. He knows how to treat sports stars. He knows how to treat carnival owners. He knows how to treat roustabouts and everyone. Tom fit with every single one of them and that was the reason he has so much love and respect in this industry."*
>
> *- Bill Alter*

Reading TP Was a Treat

People lived vicariously through the "TP on AB" column. "I feel like I'm taking a trip every week with Tom when I read his column" is a common phrase heard among AB readers.

Max Fitzpatrick is a schoolteacher from Indiana who dedicated a good portion of his life heading up the Indiana Association of County & District Fairs. In January 1997, Max wrote TP thanking him for being a friend of the fair man. "Tom, thanks for being a friend to all of us out here. We are appreciative of what you do to keep us involved and informed. We are damned envious of all the places you go, and neat things you do, but guess what? If you didn't tell us about them, and of the people connected with them, we would never get to walk that road."

Personal details, from his bowling score to his personal trips with his kids to what he had for lunch that day, were found in depth in the columns. It was amazing how his loyal readers loved to hear about TP's personal travails.

He marveled at the high tech video tape recorder he bought in 1984 and how it allowed him to not miss any of the bowl games on New Years Day. He lamented about his car troubles and informed the readers when he purchased a new car.

Those traveling abroad would write TP, tell him they were thinking of him, and more often than not, tell him they ran into someone that knew him.

Booking agent Bette Kaye took a trip to Italy in 1984 and had an audience with the Pope. She informed TP that she prayed for him and Ray Pilszak in six different Italian churches. "You have to be good now," she chided the two of them.

On one of his few trips to Germany without TP, Monsignor Robert McCarthy, The Carny Priest, better known as Father Mac, wrote back noting that "I sure miss you on these trips and try to drown my sorrows with lots and lots of beer."

> **TRUSTWORTHY**
>
> *"There is no artificial facade around Tom Powell. I always felt that this is an individual who I could confide with and he in turn could confide in me. We felt friendship and good will about each other corporately and professionally as well as individually. He is very down to earth; a real person, a fellow Pennsylvanian."*
> - Bruce McKinney, Hersheypark

About You, Not Me

Some people insist that TP's columns, especially during the earlier years were nothing but an ego-driven journal of self-gratification. Father Mac was among those most talked about in those early columns and is somewhat critical of the column.

"The people he quoted were mostly his cronies, including myself. They were the same people you would see him drinking with at the conventions and the same ones he would travel with overseas," said Father Mac. "He was comfortable with this group, they were his biggest fans. It was only natural for him to talk about them the most."

John Graff, the now retired president of the International Association of Amusement Parks and Attractions, said one has to look at the real purpose of the column. "Sure, it was a gossipy little thing filled with anecdotes. That's what made it special. I've always said the industries that AB covers are more like fraternities than economic enterprises, and his column certainly reflected that."

To enjoy "TP on AB" and to appreciate its true value, a person would have had to read it on a regular basis and be somewhat familiar with the industries and the characters. If you were only an occasional reader, it could sometimes be hard to follow. The name-dropping was usually meaningless unless you knew the people, and nobody knew as many people as TP.

Ironically, Tom once noted that those who condemned him the most for name-dropping were among the thousands each week who would read the column searching for his or her own name. Graff said he would pick the weekly issue up, scan the front news page and turn immediately to "TP on AB." Concessionaire Charlie Cox said he would scan the back page, which is the front page for carnival news, and then turn to "TP on AB."

Hey TP, Write About Me

People wanted to be mentioned and they did whatever they could to get TP's attention. Letters, jokes, photos, poems, all sorts of things arrived in the mail, with the sender hoping that TP would write about it and them. Frank Jirik of San Jose, Calif. would send bottles of California wine, others would send t-shirts, and some would actually send legitimate news items.

"When I look back now, I can only thank God there was no such thing as email, I think I would have gone crazy," TP laughs.

People were intrigued with the column because not only did it have a personality, it contained the latest update on what happened the prior week in the business. It was more current than any other trade newspaper. If something bad happened, he'd tell you about it. If something good happened, he'd tell you about it. If he had run into so and so at a fair or a carnival had a fire or somebody got hurt on one of their rides, or this fair manager is resigning or they've got a new fair manager in Ionia, Michigan, he'd tell you about it.

"He was our personal pipeline to the business. That kind of stuff is very valuable for us to know," said Tony Conway, president of Nashville-based Buddy Lee Attractions. Ray Pilszak adds: "Since his column was a direct feed to the industry, people often tried to take advantage of him. He likes people and he's empathetic with them. That makes him a softie. He's like a mark. He's a soft touch for editorial."

While never an official AB contributor, building manager George Smith provided plenty of anonymous, front line information to the publication through the years.

George Smith, alias Clark Kent, shows off new threads to TP.

TP nicknamed Smith Clark Kent in his column because he called in so many "scoops." Smith said he spent so much effort getting info to TP because he believed in both Tom and the publication.

"I always enjoyed seeing my name in his column but he tagged nicknames on many of us right from the beginning and he always called me the diminutive Dick Geyer. I'm short and he enjoyed making that an issue with me, but I didn't push the buttons because he's such a great guy and it was said in jest," said Geyer, who has managed several large facilities during his career.

Geyer said the good of being mentioned in "TP on AB" outweighed the bad. "I was in many, many times during those years and the people I met would say 'oh yeah, I read about you in TP's column' and that certainly was a plus in networking circles," Geyer said.

Bob Reid said it "certainly didn't hurt anybody's reputation" to be featured in "TP on AB." "If you had your name mentioned 15 times during the year, you were in the forefront for a lot of people within the industry. I don't think that ever hurt anybody's standing in either the industry or in the IAAM; you know, name familiarity."

Amazing Response

In an unspoken way, the column solicited letters and phone calls from the readers. Most were to inform TP of the personal side, the people-side of the industries in which he wrote about.

Retirements, transfers, births, deaths, and the like were all relayed to the industry through TP's column. If you needed to let the industry know something, getting it in the column was essential.

Sometimes it even amazed Tom at the amount of attention the column received. It seemed no matter on what subject he wrote someone identified with it and would respond. He knew his audience and he enjoyed writing to it.

Some of the correspondence was to say thank you, as did this one from Neal Gunn, then executive VP of the Houston Sports Association. "Thanks for putting my picture in the March 8 (1986) issue of the magazine. It's been a long time and I'm still ugly. Keep in touch."

Among the frivolous notes that Don Myers wrote TP through the years came this one. "My paper is always late, but I really don't care. I never let it ruin an otherwise gorgeous weekend for me."

However, some of the correspondence he received had nothing to do with what he had written in the column. Lou Harp of Fort Myers, Fla., wrote that he named an alligator Tom Powell, because "it laid around and did nothing all day." Later, John Fox of the Indiana State Fair wrote that he has "a rotten bull on the farm named Tom Powell."

To both of those, TP simply replied. "I never dreamed I would attain such distinction."

TP Fools His Readers

In an April Fool's column in 1980, TP presented an outrageous piece of "news." He reported that President Carter, in an effort to save the nation's energy, had issued an edict that said no carnivals could travel more than 200 miles from home base during 1980. Carter also allegedly said all amusement parks, shopping malls and arenas had to close during July and August, and that no hot dogs were to be sold after the third inning of any baseball game.

He closed that column by explaining that this was indeed an April Fool's prank and could only speculate how much mail he would receive if the final paragraph explaining that it was only a hoax was cut out of his column.

Hundreds of letters came in anyway; most suggesting other things President Carter should curtail. Johnny Meah, the famous show painter, wrote: "It occurred to me that this could be another Orson Welles classic, like War of the Worlds. I seem to recall that one unhinged more than a few people too." Meah sent in a cartoon he drew, and TP ran it in the column with Meah's note.

The Weekly Letter From Home

Ask and Ye Shall Receive

In 1985, he wrote that he didn't know a lot about the origin of the ever-popular Kewpie Doll, those plaster cuties handed out by the millions by carnival games operators during the first half of the 20th century. As a result of that hypothetical statement, he received letters, books, clippings, and some great personal stories about Kewpie Dolls.

He once referred to the fact that when he was working at the Scranton newspaper during his college days he would listen to baseball games in the paper's morgue, another name for a paper's library where old photos and clippings are stored.

Dozens of letters came in telling him he should have found a more appropriate place to listen to the games. "Little did I realize that most of you didn't know what a newspaper morgue was," TP wrote several weeks later. "No, I'm not THAT morbid."

"You can't say anything bad about a guy who closes each of his columns with a "God Bless," said Nashville musician and long time TP friend, Danny Davis. His first "God Bless" closing came more than six years after he began his column, on August 31, 1985. It was left off, usually dropped inadvertently by a copy editor, only a few times for the rest of the life of the column. In his column following the terrorist attacks of September 2001, he closed by adding America, to his customary God Bless.

In December 1980, he began a tradition of starting each paragraph in his last column of each year with letters that spelled out Merry Christmas All. In 1981, he felt adventurous and did a Merry Christmas And Happy New Year.

Goodbye Old Friend

"TP on AB" ran as a weekly column for the last time on October 27, 1997 and started appearing in rotation with columns written by the rest of the editorial staff, showing up every four to five weeks.

The curtain went down for good on "TP on AB," as well as all other staff columns on December 24, 2001. No one on the editorial staff knew the columns were going to be pulled.

TP's last column gave no indication that the dance was over. He started it by saying that he received the best Christmas present ever that year and it came on December 12. That's when his doctor gave him a clean bill of health from his cancer surgery. He talked about the Christmas parties he and his wife Christine attended in Nashville, and he congratulated Wayne McCary on his induction into the IAFE Hall of Fame.

The last names to appear in "TP on AB" were Neal Gunn, Mike McGee, Donna Dowless and Allen Johnson. Ticketmaster was the last company mentioned.

Approximately a year after the weekly "TP on AB" column stopped appearing, but before all staff columns were pulled, AB officials recognized a need for a more frequent column dedicated to the carnival industry. A new carnival-specific weekly column, called "On The Earie," premiered January 26, 1998.

TP recalls trying to come up with a name for the new column that would describe what it was all about. "We needed a name that would reflect the nature of the column, a weekly space that would give the news, anecdotes, rumors and the like about the carnival business and everybody connected with it," he said.

Earie is a carnival term meaning "being alert to all conversations around you, whether they are any of your business or not." On The Earie has turned out to be a popular carnival news column and has lived up nicely to its name. But it has never achieved the personality or the readership that "TP on AB" did.

Long-time friends, TP, Don Sandefur, and Jim Dalrymple.

9

THE SERIOUS MESSAGES

"TP on AB" was not always fun and frivolous. On several occasions TP used his column to share bad news with his readers, to scold industry leaders for things they shouldn't have done, and to editorialize when he felt the industry was getting the short shaft by outsiders.

His February 23, 1980 column, started out on the serious note: "I hesitate to point out that my life is not one filled only with fun and games, though this is the side I have dared to reveal so far. The places I visit are wonderful. I meet the most interesting people in the world. They're found in every phase of the business we cover. When I left the field of sports journalism it was with great hesitance because I loved writing stories about baseball, football and basketball players and boxers.

"Those stories have simply been replaced (by the industries we now cover)." But like all of you, besides laughing a lot, I cry, too. And what a shallow existence each of us would have if we never found reason to."

While experiencing what he called the joys of covering the carnival-related activities in the Tampa-Gibsonton areas of Florida, TP said he found several reasons to cry that year, some of which were too personal to mention but some of which he would share. He went on to talk about hearing of the death of his good friend Buddy Clewis.

TP used the column to discuss his various illnesses during the years and in a way, the responses he got from his friends who had or were experiencing the same problems, such as hip replacements, heart attacks, and cancer, helped TP get through his health problems. TP was always very candid about his problems.

TP ON TP

"I love my family to a fault and regret the fact my first wife and I parted. I wish I could have been able to do more for my four kids. I would like to have continued as editor of Amusement Business and I wish I were a better Catholic, person, dad, worker, and man."

- Tom Powell, on what people should know about TP

Stop The Presses

In the August 20, 1983 issue of *Amusement Business* in the spot where "TP on AB" usually ran, Publisher Howard Lander wrote a note to AB readers. "After 219 consecutive issues, nature has done what conventions, parties, vacations, time changes, foreign countries and even hangovers couldn't do - force Tom Powell to miss writing a column.

"After complaining of chest pains for more than a week, Tom consented to his doctor's advice to undergo a series of tests at Nashville's Baptist Hospital and to take a couple of weeks of well-deserved rest. To my thinking, there are no substitutes for "TP on AB." I decided against any guest columns or Notes from the Publisher. Instead we will simply place a bookmark in the issue and let the big fellow pick up where he left off."

On September 17, the big guy returned and dedicated his entire column to his heart attack, how he hadn't known it was a heart attack and that his doctors had decided not to do bypass surgery. He also explained how he didn't want anything to drink and described in graphic detail how he "upchucked" during a baseball game, a final clue that something was seriously wrong. (See more details of his heart attack in Chapter 39).

Humor is The Best Medicine

Along with the touching notes and cards, TP also received some fun and lovingly abusive comments.

Fred McCallum, who TP identified as "probably the oldest living auditorium manager," who worked at the Knoxville Civic Center, penned a note commenting on Lander's statement that the August 20 issue was the first issue published in three years with no "TP on AB." "I can't remember when I have enjoyed reading AB more (than these last three weeks)." TP commented that McCallum's note "hopefully was written tongue in cheek."

He started back to work a few hours a day a couple days a week and built back up to his manic schedule, which resumed during Country Music Week in mid-October. One thing he did do each week for sure was to write his column. He didn't miss another until the publication pulled the plug on all columns at the end of 2001.

By late October, he was still getting all kinds of letters and cards about his heart attack, some of which thanked him for describing everything so graphically. Many called it a wake-up call for themselves.

One particularly eye-catching note came from retired Admiral C.E. (Ebby) Bell, who was then director of the Norfolk, Va. Scope. "Your write-up should have done us all a great deal of good. I know I read it intently and weighed every word. I have a tendency to push myself too hard, and I hope you have helped me in stopping short of my limits. I have never known anyone who was so willing to bare his heart to the degree that you did. That may sound jocular, but it isn't meant to be. I am delighted you are

OK Tom, but from now on, give proper consideration to yourself. I don't want to see you self-destruct."

Perhaps the funniest response came in mid-November from Gene Dean who ran the Dean & Flynn Fiesta Shows in Salisbury, Beach, Mass. TP received a Western Union Telegram that read: "Dear Tom, I delayed this get-well greeting as long as possible, just to make sure you are going to recover. No sense in sending flowers twice."

John Wood of Sally Corp. in Jacksonville, Fla., wrote "You get more mileage out of life than do 99.9% of us. Here's to the marathon man. Keep on running!"

Three years later he was still getting calls about his health. Milt Kaufman of Gooding's Million Dollar Midways called and said that he had heard via the grapevine "that you're not taking care of yourself and have put back on a lot of weight." Of course, TP asked where he had heard that and Kaufman stayed true to the carny code. "I'm no stool pigeon, but we want you around writing "TP on AB" for another 70 years."

Nearly four years after TP's heart attack, Father Mac wrote him a note. "You are a living example that heart attacks are not fatal! Every time I read about you playing ball, I am amazed and think of how you have recovered with all our prayers and how you have not let it get you down."

A Dear Friend's Passing

Another heart-felt expression of love and loss appeared in fall, 1983 shortly after Rosamond, his first wife who he had divorced in 1972, died of cancer. They became friends again after "some of the much justified bitterness on her part subsided," he said. "We became better friends than we had ever been during a marriage that began in 1957."

John Hobbs, TP, Willie Nelson and Buddy Lee.

He explained in his column that they had become very close during the last few years of her life and she was the first one who had visited him in the hospital after his heart attack. TP was back living in her house at the time of her death, with her mother preparing meals "and making me feel as though I had never been gone, as if I belonged."

He openly wished that his many friends in the industry could have had an opportunity to meet her. "She would have liked you. You would have loved her! I did!"

He spoke of Rosamond again in his November 21, 1987 column when he announced the upcoming marriage of his youngest daughter, Alice. She was the first of his and Rosamond's four children to get married.

"It was 30 years ago November 9 that I was lucky enough to wed her mom. Alice will be wearing the same dress. It fits her like a glove and I know I'm going to have a hard time walking down that aisle with such a beautiful lady for the second time," he wrote.

In March 1997, TP said goodbye to his brother Bob who died of cancer at 58 years old. TP had visited him, been able to hug and say his final goodbyes just prior to Bob's death. "I loved him with all my heart, and wish I had told him that more when he could have heard it," he wrote.

TP was informed of his brother's death the same day he was diagnosed with walking pneumonia, which made it impossible for him to attend his brother's funeral. TP says it hurt bad not to be able to attend, but that he had been lucky to spend three days with him several weeks before.

TP and his brother Bob Powell.

10

MEETING, LOVING, LOSING & WINNING CHRISTINE

Tom walked down the aisle again in 1991 with another beautiful woman, Christine Reid, a carnival concessionaire he had known for 15 years.

TP remembers the 1976 convention of the International Association of Amusement Parks & Attractions in New Orleans as the event where he "met the nicest person" he had ever known. What started out as just another closing banquet at the convention, turned out to be a night that changed TP's life forever.

The band played, people were dancing, eating and laughing. Christine Reid didn't have a ticket to the banquet but wanted to see the band that was playing. She asked her friend, Jack Kaplan to sneak her up to the balcony overlooking the floor so she could watch.

"I looked down and there at the side of the floor sat Tom Powell, all by himself with his bottle of Scotch," Christine, now Mrs. Tom Powell, remembers. That evening, she met Tom and Mr. Scotch at the same time. She had heard of him and was a subscriber to *Amusement Business*, but she says she "hadn't been reading the paper long enough to be real impressed upon meeting him."

Kaplan introduced the two and during the evening kept coming up and introducing Tom to other people, one person after another. "All night long he just kept coming by and bringing people. He'd come by and say, 'Tom Powell, editor of Billboard meet so and so.' And you know Tom would stand up and speak and I thought that sooner or later this guy is going to blow. He's going to get so tired of this, but he was such a character and never was anything less than a gentleman."

TP is Smitten

Between interruptions, Christine and Tom sat there all evening watching the entertainment and getting to know each other. He drank his Scotch, she drank Crown Royal and they danced a little and talked a lot.

"We sat and talked for hours. I remember going back to the room I was sharing with Steve Rogers, our managing editor and telling him that I had just met the nicest person I had ever met in my life," recalls Tom.

She sent him a Christmas card and he called her. Then nothing happened for awhile.

"I was playing a spot in Arcadia, Fla. and he was going to be in Miami. He called and said he would come by and see me but he didn't show up. Then I saw him in Las Vegas a couple weeks later. He asked me to have a drink. He didn't show up again, but of course I didn't either so it didn't matter," Christine laughed.

Obviously, she wasn't too impressed with who he was, but she was attracted to him. "I probably was most impressed with his personality, right from the beginning," she recalls. "That first night, how he totally kept his composure. That really impressed me." Two months later he asked her to go to the banquet with him at the Gibsonton trade show, and that's when the "official" dating process began, four months after their first meeting.

On The Road With Christine

Christine ran a food stand and traveled with various carnivals. She sold Polish sausage, Italian sausage, hamburgers, hot dogs, corn dogs, cold drinks, and was on the road for a great deal of the year. TP was a good guy to get to know for a woman in her line of work. He had a lot of contacts in the business, even back then.

"She wasn't doing too well on the Canadian route she was working, so I was able to get her booked with Rod Link on his carnival. He put her in a

TP and Christine pose with Roy Rogers. Country singer Jim Ed Brown looks on from the background.

front location with that small joint and in 10 days she grossed $30,000 and netted $18,000 at the State Fair of Oklahoma.

The next week she went to the Alabama State Fair in Birmingham. She grossed $18,000 and netted $12,000. In 20 days she made $30,000, according to TP.

One of the earliest spots Christine played with Link was in Columbia, Tenn., about 40 miles from Nashville, where TP was based. It was Labor Day weekend and TP thought it would be a good opportunity to spend some time with her.

"When I got there she was doing so much business she immediately asked me to take her pickup truck and go to the grocery store and get all the ice I could get, and I did. I came back and she sent me right back to get all the ice I could get again. She took in over $3,000 that day."

During those months, TP spent as much time with Christine as possible. He tried to make sure his business trips would take him near to where Christine was working.

"He used to come in quite often, like every weekend. But when he came to visit he didn't just come in and stay with me. He would visit other carnivals and arenas, whatever was around," Christine recalls.

"I discovered carnivals out there that we didn't know existed," TP said. He was also quite popular with the kids of the carnival workers. He would take some of the carny kids with him if he were going to a park or another carnival.

At other times, he would lend a hand in Christine's food trailer and she remembers that Rod Link would visit "just to get his jollies for the day while watching Tom try to make foot-long hotdogs while the buns kept breaking in his hand. I finally put him in charge of cash. He does much better counting money than preparing food."

Now What Do I Do?

Christine points out a time when Tom was more willing than able to help out. "One day in Oklahoma City, our biggest spot, we had really been jammed up and had lots of help problems. One morning Tom says 'today is kind of a slow day. Why don't you just sleep in a little bit. I'll go down and open up the joint,' and I knew that Lumpy, my regular helper would be there as well, so I wasn't worried."

As luck would have it, Lumpy chose that day to not show up. "Tom goes down to open up the stand and he can't find Lumpy. This lady who had been working for me all week comes in and all she sees is Tom there, and she's like where's Ms. Christine and Tom says 'she'll be here later. I'm going to let her sleep in.' She says 'you mean it's just you and me here?' Tom says 'yeah.' She says 'well I'm leaving. I'm not staying here with just you unless Ms. Christine gets here.'"

Realizing he could be in deep trouble, he went back, woke up Christine proclaiming that "all I know how to do is make coffee."

See You Later

The long distance relationship didn't last for more than three years. Christine ended up getting married to someone else for a short time, but the two remained friends and would talk to each other at conventions and when they ran into each other on the road.

Ironically, it was back in New Orleans, where they had first met, that the two got back together 11 years later, at another amusement park convention. Tom likes to kid that Christine "came crawling back" on her hands and knees. "Luckily I was still available. Oddly enough I never stopped loving her and we now have a great life. I take her everywhere I go."

She moved to Nashville in 1990 and they got married in 1991. "Let me tell you about the day they got married," said Nashville Palace owner John Hobbs who was TP's best man. "They kept putting it off. I said you're living in sin. You need to get married. I can't stand anybody that's single and happy. You've got to get married and suffer. So they decided to get married. I called Bill Covington, the county court clerk. He issues marriage licenses and he can marry you and I arranged everything with him," Hobbs explains.

"On Friday, we get in the car and leave Tom's house heading to the county clerk's office. There was me, my wife Libby, Tom and Christine. It started storming. It was the damndest storm you ever saw. I said, Tom, this may be telling you not to get married. We get to Bill's office and they get ready to get married and the clerk asks them for the rings. They didn't bring any.

"Tom looks at Christine and says I gave you a diamond 10 years ago, where is it? She digs through her purse and finds an old ring and gave it to me as the best man. Tom didn't have one so I took my wedding band off and give it to Christine to use for the service. Meanwhile, Bill Covington was about ready to crack a gut. He's in the middle of the ceremony and couldn't keep from laughing."

Hey Karen, I Got Married!

Later that afternoon, TP called Karen Oertley, AB Publisher to tell her that he had gotten married. She was in Atlanta at the Fun Expo family entertainment center tradeshow and was getting ready to leave for a World Series Game.

"Tom calls and I'm in my hotel room and he goes 'are you sitting down' and I said, oh, no, what happened? So he goes, 'no, no, nothing bad, I just wanted to let you know that I married Christine this afternoon and I wanted you to be one of the first to know.' I think the world of Christine and think she's the best thing that ever happened to Tom. I knew her when they dated years before and I was happy they got back together and married." Oertley congratulated him and headed off to the game wondering what she would get him for a wedding gift.

Oertley ran into TP's friend Tommy Lasorda in the press box at the

World Series and the two chatted for a few minutes and she told him about Tom and Christine. Then she got an idea. "You know there's really nothing I can give Tom as a wedding present so would you call his voicemail at work and leave him a message telling him congratulations, and that could be my gift to Tom."

Lasorda happily obliged and called Tom on his office phone and being late at night, voicemail answered. Lasorda did his Rodney Dangerfield routine like, "Hey, Tom, how did she (Christine) get to like you. Is she blind or what? Did you meet her at the Braille Institute?" Tom was surprised and excited about the message and got his son Kevin to make a copy of the recording so he was able to save it.

> **BIG HELP**
>
> *"He does absolutely nothing around the house. Well, once in a while he will change the thermostat."*
>
> *- Christine Powell*

Thanks for Coming Back, Christine

John Hobbs points out that Christine came back into TP's life at the right time and thinks she has prolonged TP's life by doing so.

"I don't think he could live without her. Tom has to have somebody drive for him and help him do a lot of things. You know, Tom's 70 years old. Everybody slows down when you get that age. And today Tom, with two hip replacements and leg problems, can't even put on his socks. He's always getting somebody to put his socks on for him. And without Christine I don't know what he'd do. He has to have somebody. He can't pick up his own clothes."

Concessionaire Bill Lordy, owner of the Elephant Ear Bakery, said if Christine ever left TP, he would never wear socks again. "He depends on her to put his socks on and when she isn't around, which is rare, he'll go out not wearing socks but will have a pair in his pocket to put on when he finds someone to help. I did it once, but told him never again," laughed Lordy.

Target of The Fashion Police

"When you get down to common sense Tom doesn't know which pair of pants goes with what or what suspenders goes with what," Hobbs said. "He'd be lost. He'd probably come in with yellow suspenders and a purple shirt or something. She takes good care of him and looks after him and worries about him a lot. They really do love each other. He picks on her a lot and makes her mad but they get back real quick."

Long time friend Don Sandefur thinks marriage has tempered Tom. "She treats him great. Unbelievable. There must be a lot of love there because she puts up with a lot."

Another friend, Thaxter Trafton agrees that Christine is the best thing to ever happen to him. "If ever a person could come onto this earth and stabilize Tom, it would certainly be her, he loves her dearly."

"Tom is one of the luckiest guys in the world because he married Christine," adds Bill Lordy. "She is many valuable things to TP; his lover, his chauffeur, his go-for, and his personal secretary. Tom is a bit klutzy and is not really productive unless he has a pen, notepad and computer. Christine is a big help for everything else."

"There is no doubt Christine is the best thing that ever happened to Tom. She's done a lot of good for *Amusement Business* as well. She carries the camera and takes care of a lot of things that he can't do," notes Publisher Oertley.

> **FATHER MOWS BEST**
>
> *"Tom says he used to mow the lawn, but I can't find any neighbors who ever saw him do it. His kids don't remember it either."*
> *- Christine Powell*

CP on AB

There could easily be another column in *Amusement Business* called Christine Powell on AB. Through the years she has gotten to know nearly as many people as Tom, and has helped him gather the news as well as any cub reporter could.

She'll stay in the booth with him at conventions, travel with him from one fair to another and sit for hours with him as he interviews subjects from all walks of life. She does it because she enjoys it and she loves him, but she also does it because TP physically needs her by his side.

"I have to plug in the computer and I have to dress him in the morning. But, it's a wonderful life and I like sharing it with him."

Tom will show up at the AB booth at a convention and sit down at a table. Christine, knowing the industries and the people so well, goes out and brings people back to the booth for TP to interview.

One of Christine's friends at the Gibsonton carnival trade show recently made a crack to her that they had a "neat" deal worked out. Tom just sits there and does his stories and Christine's out in the aisles calling them in. "I said well I'm a carny. I know how to do that. I'm just calling them in for him."

Christine has also learned to take pictures and will often pick up TP's camera and go off and shoot some photos. "I might point out that some of the best pictures in AB are by Christine," she laughed.

TP working Christine's joint at the State Fair of Oklahoma.

11

A SERIES OF SUPER BOWLS

After coming to work for *Amusement Business*, Tom didn't have as many opportunities to meet and interview sports celebrities as he had when he worked as a sports reporter. However, at AB he had many different and even bigger sports-related opportunities. He was able to attend the largest of all sporting events, in the name of work and without an immediate deadline.

In his new journalistic role, his job was to interview the stadium or arena managers about the business side of the sport, not the athletes themselves about the playing of the game. He was now more interested in finding out about stadium operations, ticket sales and concession sales than batting averages or first downs.

Tom has attended more than 20 Super Bowls since joining AB, mostly in the company of Ray Pilszak and Howard Lander. At those games, however, TP was much more than another fan in the stands or another journalist in the press box.

He was treated special wherever he went. TP was the guest of Baron Hilton at pre-game parties and was included as a VIP in the special lounges and suites both before and after the games. He knew the top management of the stadium where the game was being played, he knew the manager of the stadium's food service company, the top officials of the merchandise company, and the security company. He was treated as royalty and with all those contacts, he had the run of the stadium.

The first Super Bowl the three attended was at the Cliff Wallace-run Louisiana Superdome in New Orleans in 1981. Tom's favorite NFL team the Philadelphia Eagles was in it for the first time playing against the Oakland Raiders. Wallace invited the three of them to the game and it didn't take long for them to accept the invitation.

Lander had just been made publisher and in that role, he informed the guys before they left that since the outing had nothing to do with AB coverage, they would all be paying for it on their own.

No Rooms on The Bayou

There were no hotel rooms available in the city by the time they received the invitation, so Wallace offered to put them up in his home. The real adventure however, started when the three climbed into the car in Nashville to head south to New Orleans.

Lander picks up the story. "Ray was driving and he wouldn't stop, and we were starved. We kept saying, Ray, you've got to find a place to eat. It's getting late. Ray was just so stubborn about it. Finally he pulls into some truck stop. We had a great meal and we got a room at a motel down the road. We shared one room because we wanted to save money. We get to the room and there are only two beds but I'm the publisher so I said I'm taking one bed and the two of you can stay in another bed or sleep on the floor. I don't care."

It was a cold night and they couldn't figure out how to fix the heat in the room. "We're laying there pissing and moaning and freezing. We all wanted to fall quickly asleep because the whole idea when you're traveling with Tom is to fall asleep before he does or otherwise with his snoring you're never going to go sleep."

At the game, the three ran into arena managers, stadium managers, and food guys from all corners of the country. Of course TP had his camera and was taking pictures of everybody. Within five minutes they ran into three AB subscribers: Johnny Hardeman who was scalping tickets, Ron Wigmore, the president of the IAAM, and carnival owner Art Frazier."

> **TP ON TP**
>
> *"I would enjoy myself, just as I do every day now with wife, Christine. I'd go back to Scranton where I was born and hang around with guys I grew up with."*
> *- Tom Powell on what he would do if his days on earth were numbered.*

Two weeks after returning to Nashville, Lander told Pilszak and TP that since AB was trying to get in tighter with arenas and stadiums, and since there had been so many industry people at the game, that AB would pick up the tab for the trip. He also announced that from then on, Super Bowl trips were legitimate business trips.

A String of Super Bowls

Don Sandefur was working for the Harlem Globetrotters in Los Angeles in 1983, and Super Bowl XVII, with Miami playing Washington was set to take place in the Rose Bowl in nearby Pasadena.

TP, Lander and Pilszak journeyed to Los Angeles and Sandefur picked them up at the airport. The following day, after the game, he surprised them by taking them to the Lobster Barrel Restaurant, which was owned by a friend of his, Allen Hale Jr., the actor who played the skipper on "Gilligan's Island."

That evening turned out to be a high point of the weekend for everyone. "Allen sat there and told all these stories to Tom, Howard and Ray.

They were a great audience for Allen and he talked about all the old television shows and the movies he'd been in and, hell, I mean we stayed there until they closed and Allen still wasn't ready to let them go. It was a lot of fun. Then I took the photo of the Skipper and Tom and Ray and it appeared in AB," Sandefur said, noting that TP didn't give him photo credit.

Through Dark Glasses

Held in late January each year, Super Bowl usually came at the end of a long month of travel for TP, Lander and Pilszak. Most often, the three would be attending an industry trade show in Germany and visiting ride factories in other European countries the week prior to the big game. They would fly back to the states and head directly to the host city.

In 1985 the three attended their fifth straight Super Bowl. That year it took place in what TP refers to as one of the "most amateurish, ill-prepared facilities in the country," Stanford University Stadium, in Palo Alto, Calif.

Maybe one of the reasons for his dim view of the stadium was the fact that he had to wear sunglasses. He had broken his glasses in Germany and only had prescription sun glasses to wear, if he wanted to see anything.

"Thank God they were prescription, or I wouldn't have been able to see even the shadows of the players," he noted. Following the game, the three got lost trying to find their car and TP struggled to keep up and to see where he was going. "Ray mercilessly taunted me at one point, when I crashed a shin into a fire plug that I couldn't see," TP remembers.

A souvenir from Super Bowl XXIX.

Trying out Peter Petz's custom carousel at the amusement park convention.

12

TP MEETS HIS SPORTS HEROES

Today, TP is most associated with the carnival industry, but he first made his name at *Amusement Business* covering the area of facility management.

As part of its arena, stadium, and building coverage, AB covered the business side of sports for several years in the late 1980s to the mid-1990s. Of course, as a trained sports journalist, TP was in his full glory.

Tom brought experience and background to AB that helped create unique people and business-oriented sports coverage that set the newspaper apart from its competition.

At *The Tennessean*, Nashville's daily newspaper, his first official beat was auto racing and he covered every Daytona 500 from 1958 through 1972. "They gave me Indianapolis 500 and that became my specialty. I never became a racing fan, but I learned to like the people. I wrote mostly about people. I wrote about them the way I write about anything else and I really didn't need to know the technicalities of the sport."

That focus on people is what sets TP's writing apart from all others who had written for *Amusement Business* in the past. He brought a fresh personal approach to writing when he joined the paper.

Heaven for a Baseball Fan

The first World Series TP covered was while he was still working for *The Tennessean*, a year before joining AB. It was the 1971 series between the Baltimore Orioles and the Pittsburgh Pirates. Sometime between picking up his tickets, field, dugout and clubhouse passes and the time he was to leave for the first game, all his credentials disappeared.

"I didn't have the heart to tell anybody and was a bit embarrassed, but I didn't know what to do," he said. He literally tore up his room looking for them and as he was leaving to sign up for replacement credentials, he saw a maid in the hallway, explained what was missing and asked if she had seen them when she had cleaned the room. She didn't remember, but offered to help hunt. They dumped out the vacuum bag and they dumped out the trash bags and got on their hands and knees digging through the rubble. They found them.

"Can you imagine what the odds were for that maid to be in that spot at that precise time and then to actually find them? It's amazing," he said.

> **SIMILARITIES**
>
> *"TP reminds me of baseball great Babe Ruth. Not only because of their matching girth, but because TP has swung at a few bad pitches through the years but overall he's been a good hitter."*
>
> *- Thaxter Trafton*

All-Time Favorites

Today, TP is hard pressed to come up with a list of his all time favorite sporting events. However, when asked what event was the most exciting for him, he has no problem citing the Ali-Frazier fight at Madison Square Garden in 1971 as "the biggest thrill" of his life.

Additional thrills that come to his mind are the interviews he had with both Ted Williams and Joe DiMaggio within days of each other. Williams was and still is TP's all-time sports hero, and he had a chance to meet him when the hero came to Nashville.

As he was preparing to interview the icon, he was concerned that Williams would be a jerk and that TP's bubble would be burst. "I was so afraid Ted might not be nice to me but it turned out that he couldn't have been nicer." When the official interview was over and the two started talking about baseball in general, William's people urged him to hurry because they were already late for another event where he was scheduled to speak.

When they began encouraging Williams to leave, TP got up and thanked Williams for the interview. "Sit down," Williams said. He then told his handlers that he was having a good time. "I'm talking to a baseball man here and I'm enjoying it."

TP calls baseball great Stan Musial a friend. It all started when Tom was curious about who was subscribing to AB. He looked over the subscription list and surprisingly saw Musial's name. Out of curiosity he called the slugger to find out why he liked reading *Amusement Business*.

He didn't get through right away, but Musial's people said he would get back to TP as soon as possible. He hung up wondering if he would ever hear from the guy. Several days later, Tom came to work and checked his voice messages. "Hi Tom, this is Stan the Man. How about calling me back about 4 o'clock, around cocktail hour?"

He called back and they talked for nearly an hour. "First of all he said he enjoyed reading my column. In addition to baseball, he owned a novelty store business. Another guy ran it but it was Musial's merchandise, and he said he found AB very useful for that. I said I'd like to get together with him and he said to call him sometime."

It didn't take TP long to find an excuse to get to St. Louis. He called Musial and set up a lunch with him at the Stouffer Airport Hotel. Nashville friends John and Libby Hobbs and former Nashville councilman Guy Bates and his wife Clara joined Christine and Tom.

"We're waiting for him at the restaurant and in walks this guy with a ball cap with long hair and a ponytail attached to it. He came in a side door with a big smile on his face, came right over and grabbed and hugged us all," TP remembers. "He said this is for you, Tom. He played "When Irish Eyes Are Smiling" on his harmonica. He had autographed baseballs for all of us. That's how classy he was."

As Musial got up to leave, he told TP. "My good friend Jim Michener the great author, always says that at our age, any day you wake up is a good one. He also says if you love somebody, you should tell them." Musial then gave TP a big bear hug and said, "Tom, we love you."

> **THE RIGHT MAN**
>
> *"I always said Tom Powell was the perfect editor for AB in the 80's. I could never have turned it into one of the most profitable publications BPI had if it hadn't been for TP. His personality and his people-skills brought a great bit of attention to the magazine. Circulation was at the all-time high, advertising sales were good. It was just the right time."*
> -Howard Lander, AB Publisher

A Friend of Cassius

Always a big boxing fan, TP was delighted to have the opportunity to meet and eventually become relatively close to one of the greatest fighters of all times. "I interviewed Cassius Clay about 50 times before he became Muhammed Ali. We became great friends."

The fighter came to Nashville often and when he did, TP would usually be tipped off that he was in town. "I would get a call at 1 or 2 in the morning from a guy telling me that he was over on Jefferson Street, in the middle of the black community. Of course I'd go visit, but I'd be nervous until I'd see him and he would smile and start spouting all that poetry to me."

However, over the years TP saw Clay's attitude change and one night he confronted the fighter. TP says Cassius Clay had been the most delightful person until he became Muhammad Ali. That's when he started having all the bodyguards with him and it was a totally different environment around the fighter.

"I had just read an article on Malcolm X where Muslims didn't do any hanky panky. One night I saw a guy going up and whispering to him that he had a girl back in the room for him, and I couldn't resist saying something. The one white guy in the middle of all these big black guys and for some reason I had the nerve to speak out." As usual, TP didn't pull any punches. "I said you're a hypocrite. You talk about being a devout Muslim.

I said I had heard the comment about a woman being in his room. He just exploded. He said 'I don't wear robes and I come out among my people. Joe Louis never came out among his people. I'm here and I'm not a saint.'" That was one of the last meetings between the two.

> **SURFER TOM**
>
> "I gave Tom a special television package that features hundreds of different channels. More importantly, it televises just about every baseball game. The first thing in the morning he checks to see how many games are on and he bases his work and play schedule around the games he wants to watch."
>
> - Christine Powell

The Best Stories Ever Written

A highlight of his *Tennessean* newspaper days was when he interviewed Cassius Clay before he became Muhammad Ali, and Tennessee Olympic star Wilma Rudolph within hours of each other. He thinks the stories he wrote on both that day rank as two of the best stories he has ever written.

At that time, the city side reporters of *The Tennessean* didn't think too highly of the sports reporters. "They always thought we were the toy department down on the second floor in sports, and they kind of looked down their noses at us." But to his surprise, many of the "real" reporters came down and complimented him on those two stories. His sense of accomplishment ended rather quickly when he was called into the managing editor's office. Expecting further kudos from this "man of stature at the newspaper had been the head of the Associated Press before joining the daily," TP had a big smile as he entered the inner sanctum of the newspaper.

"I walked in expecting to be complimented and he showed me the paper with a lot of things marked on it and he said, 'son, I want you to know one thing. We're not putting out a nigger newspaper here.' I thought, welcome to the Deep South, Tom."

For several years while he was a sports writer at *The Tennessean*, the paper sponsored the Golden Gloves Association. The sports editor Raymond Johnson headed up the mid-state Golden Gloves and got TP involved. When Johnson died, a Jewish doctor in Nashville, Sam Bernow who had earlier boxed as Irish Eddy Burke took over. When he got older, he handed the leadership over to TP in the mid-1960s.

During that time Tom was approached to promote a professional fight between Nashvillian Billy Collins and Birmingham native Guy Sumlin in Nashville. Tom thought it would be a good marketing ploy to get former champion Jack Dempsey as judge. Without much trouble, he was able to get in touch with Dempsey and talked him into coming to Nashville for the match.

"I spent a whole day with Dempsey and still kick myself that I didn't get a picture made with him, an autograph, or anything." TP did get a personal insight into the fighter's past. "He told me a million stories. In the older days, he would go into a town and beat up the toughest guy, make a few bucks, and then would hop a freight train with his manager Jack (Doc) Kearns and move to the next town. I spent a lot of time with him and really enjoyed every minute of it."

Another Special Baseball Moment

While working at *The Tennessean*, TP briefly met Joe DiMaggio in Nashville in the 1960s. He saw him again at an International Association of Assembly Managers' convention in the late 1970s. "I went over and talked to him for about 10 minutes and we were reminiscing about baseball during the 50's. I knew every guy on the Red Sox and Yankees teams and apparently he appreciated that I knew what I was talking about and we had a good time talking baseball.

"I was monopolizing too much of his time and it wasn't fair to others waiting to talk with him. I said I had to go and I started to leave. He says 'where are you going?' Obviously he didn't want me to leave. He was enjoying it as much as I was. I stammered, I said I've got to get back to my booth. I didn't have to get back just then but I was so shocked that he wanted me to stay that was the best I could come up with."

Super Time @ The Superdome

TP visited the Louisiana Superdome in New Orleans in 1993 to watch an exhibition game between his beloved Red Sox and the New York Yankees. As usual, he had total access to the field and the press box. George Steinbrenner, the Yankee's owner, and his manager, Bucky Showalter, were standing on the edge of the field before the game and Tom walked over, introduced himself and chatted with the two for awhile.

"It was exciting to meet both of them, but my real thrill of the day was going up to the press box and running into Mel Parnell, the best left-handed pitcher in the history of the Red Sox. I also met John Harrington, the president of the Red Sox."

For years, TP and Johnny Hobbs, his best friend from Nashville would go up to South Bend, Indiana a couple of times each fall for a Notre Dame football game, usually as the guest of mutual friend Joe Sassano, who ran the sports venues at the university. It was Sassano who introduced TP to football coach Lou Holtz and the two have forged a relationship over the years.

Sassano has gotten TP into many events at the school over the years and has introduced him to a lot of people. Every year TP is invited, along with the top members of the national press, to media day activities where they see a scrimmage, have dinner, and meet the players and the coaches. As an

Irish fan, TP always looks forward to that invitation.

Tom visited his first NBA All-Star game in Seattle in 1987, with his long time friend Thaxter Trafton who was then president of the Cleveland Cavaliers NBA team. The two walked into the Kingdome and Thaxter recognized David Stern, the NBA commissioner, walking toward them.

"I asked Tom if he had ever met David Stern, he said no. I asked if he would like to meet him and he beamed all over," Trafton recalls. "We walked up and I said David, I would like for you to meet a friend of mine, Tom Powell of *Amusement Business*." He smiled and stuck out his hand to shake TP's hand. "I recognize Tom Powell. I read his column every week," Stern said.

John Friedmann and TP.

"That was one of only a few times I ever saw TP stumped for words," Trafton noted. "After that, he wanted me to take him around and introduce him to others. I laughed when he asked me and told him everyone would probably wonder who that guy is with Tom Powell."

A Little Help From a Friend

Tom was in Kansas City in the late 90's visiting with his friend John Friedmann. He mentioned that while he was in Kansas City that he would like to meet Dick Schultz, the head of the NCAA, which had offices in nearby Overland Park. Friedmann had gotten to know Schultz from the NCAA Final Four in 1988, which was held in the Friedmann-managed Kemper Arena.

"We were just sitting there and Tom had no idea that I knew Schultz. He said do you suppose he would see me if I went over to visit him. I said sure, Tom, and I picked up the phone, called him, arranged for a meeting and we went. Of course Tom had his camera and got some great photos during that visit."

Tom Hasn't Met Everyone Yet

In early 2003, Trafton was talking on the phone with Pat Gallagher, president of the San Francisco Giants. "As we were talking, Pat mentioned that he would someday like to meet a friend of mine. I had no idea where he was going with this, and it turned out to be TP. 'I would love to meet that guy,' Pat told me. He is well known in sports all over the country, yet he would be as interested in meeting Tom as I'm sure Tom would be in meeting him."

13

TP COACHES THE GLOBETROTTERS

Carnival owner Bud Gilmore and TP traveled to the Final Four NCAA basketball tournament in Indianapolis at the Hoosier Dome. Through TP's connections the two had seats reserved in a suite.

As usual, TP had his camera over his shoulder as they walked into the building. Officials stopped him and told him that no cameras were allowed. Gilmore said that at the point of nearly having his camera confiscated, TP showed true prowess.

"They were going to take it away from him so he turned around and left. He knew the people that ran the food service there, so he got in touch with them, gave them the camera and we went on up to the suite. A few minutes later, food service arrived with his camera hidden in one of their carts. He got his camera and he got his pictures, and did his stories and we sat there and watched the game and had a great time," Gilmore recalls.

In 1982, TP realized another dream, thanks to Don Sandefur, operations director for the Harlem Globetrotters. Sandefur recalls a fun evening in Nashville. Tom and Howard Lander had always talked about how great it would be if they could sit on the bench with the Harlem Globetrotters. When the opportunity presented itself in Nashville, Sandefur stepped forward. "I said I could have one guy on one bench and one on the other. Since both Howard and Red Klotz, the owner and the coach of the Washington Generals, the team that plays the Globetrotters, are from New Jersey I put Howard with them. I put Tom on the Globetrotter's bench."

Both were made honorary coaches for the night and were introduced to the crowd before the game. Sandefur had a Globetrotter jacket made up with Coach Tom Powell written in scroll. After a Globetrotters game, kids are invited to come onto the floor, meet the players and get autographs. That night, they also went up to Tom. "Coach, coach, give me your autograph," the kids kept saying.

Sandefur recalls that TP was in his prime that evening. "He's out in the middle of the floor and he's signing autographs and every time he starts walking away, the kids would follow him wanting his autograph. It was just unbelievable at the number of kids and I bet Tom signed autographs for 20 minutes."

TP was amazed at the throng of both adults and kids that surrounded the players after the game. One frustrated father who had been standing with his son waiting for a player's autograph finally pointed to Tom standing there and told his son. "You might as well go over there and get his signature. He's the owner of the team."

For the next three years, when the Globetrotters came to town, TP and Lander assumed their coaching responsibilities. However, on January 1, 1983, they both had to chip in and do a little work before the afternoon game at Municipal Auditorium. Due to the New Year's holidays, advanced sales for the game were down, but the walk-up that day was huge and Sandefur was pressed into action selling tickets, with Lander and TP sitting next to him making change.

TP Time at The Masters

Having been to virtually every other major sporting event in America during his life, TP had never attended the Masters Championship in Augusta, Ga. In 1995, thanks to an invitation from carnival owner Jimmy Drew of the James H. Drew Exposition, he got to go. Drew, an Augusta native acquired some tickets and sent TP and Christine off to the big event with these words. "Remember, the worst golfer you see playing here will probably be the best you ever saw."

Playing in his first Masters that year was Tiger Woods, then a freshman student at Stanford University. Standing at the 9th hole, TP first saw the great Jack Nicklaus play through, then Woods. With incredible luck, TP saw history in the making. In his column the following week, he reported, "Now, when Tiger becomes one of the greatest players of all times, as he's destined to be, I can say I saw him play in his first Masters!" Little did he know.

The Skywriter's Tour

As a sports writer for *The Tennessean*, TP covered mostly Ohio Valley Conference and Southeast Conference sports. Each year, he took part in the annual Skywriter's Tour, a yearly journey through the 12 conference schools of the SEC. One of his most memorable stops one year was at the University of Alabama where he had the opportunity to meet and interview Coach Bear Bryant.

He liked Bryant and gets riled when people call him a racist or say that Bryant was part of a regime that oppressed blacks. "People don't remember that was just the way it was done in those days. It wasn't Bryant's fault. On one trip, a wise ass reporter from Florida says to Bryant, 'how come until last year you never had any black football players?' I thought Bryant was brilliant in his answer. He didn't hesitate. He said, 'Son, until last year it just wasn't the thing to do around here.' That's it you know. It wasn't his fault. That's just the way life was."

The Firecracker 400

TP covered every Daytona auto race between 1958 and 1972 and of all the interviews he conducted, he was most impressed with Richard Petty, a driver he calls a real class act. "I had an interview with Petty, a long interview on a tape recorder. As I was walking away, the tape got caught on something and became unraveled. He saw it happen and says, 'Tom, you lost the interview. Come on back and we'll do it again.' You'll never find a guy nowadays who would do that. He was the king then, the #1 driver."

Los Angeles Dodgers' Manager and Baseball Hall of Fame member Tommy Lasorda and TP.

TP meets musician Al Hirt.

14

EVEN TP CAN'T WIN THEM ALL

TP loves to not only watch sports, but to wager on the games as well. Unfortunately, he usually doesn't have much luck.

Long-time friend Bill Alter points out that Tom certainly isn't the lucky Irishman when it comes to betting. "We all know that Tom has had a long time arrangement with several local bookies in Nashville. In fact if I recall correctly he has outlived three different bookies.

"I laugh at his betting skills because he always comes across as so sure of being able to pick the winners, but in the end I have only known Tom to say he actually collected money one time. When the bookie visits it's to collect not to pay off," Alter notes.

David Smith, now president of Allied Specialty Insurance, remembers that his late father, Duke Smith and TP were not only the best of friends, but they shared Mr. Mel Barnes, a "sports auditor," a word they chose to use instead of bookie.

Smith recalls one particular instance that pretty much defines TP's skills at wagering. "We were at the office one Saturday and Tom called Duke and they started going over a bunch of bets that Tom was getting ready to place. Duke wrote Tom's choices down and he was giggling the entire time Tom was talking. He hung up the phone, called his bookie and bet every game the opposite of what Tom bet, and he won. He did that for several years. Then he just quit talking to Tom first and would call their bookie, and tell him that he wanted to bet opposite of whatever Tom bet."

Let's Skip the Sports Auditor

Duke called Tom one day and said, "Listen Tom, why do we even screw with the bookie. Why don't you just pay me the money." TP never talks about his wins or his losses but he does admit that he seldom collects. He's also quick to point out that he always pays his debts. "Nobody has ever come looking for me, that's for sure. I always pay off."

Tom thinks he has it figured out why he doesn't win very often. "I bet with my heart. I'll never bet against a team that I'm rooting for. In other words, I would never bet against Notre Dame or Penn State. Now that doesn't mean I'm going to bet on them but I would never bet against them."

He can't understand how weekend warriors who play in the fantasy baseball leagues do so well. "In most cases they don't know beans about baseball and I'm like an expert. I read every box score every day and when I played in the fantasy league for several years, I finished last every season."

One bet he would always make was on the Kentucky Derby. Debbie Burda of the Kentucky Fair & Exposition Center in Louisville, creates a friendly pool each year for the industry that lives outside the area but wants to make a $2 bet on the Derby. Unlike AB's Ray Pilszak, who always seems to win something every time he bets, TP finally brought in the winnings when he bet on Sunday Silence in the 1989 Derby. He picked up $8.20 that afternoon, and he made it a point to put it in his column the following week to let everyone know that even TP can win a bet now and then.

His personal throne at Gibtown.

15

ALWAYS HELPS TO KNOW THE BAR KEEP

TP was working at *The Tennessean* newspaper, along with three other jobs when he first met his good buddy, John Hobbs.

They both belonged to the Knights of Columbus and would end up at all the parties together. That's how they got to know each other and they soon found they had a strong bond between them. They both loved to drink, talk and party.

Hobbs owns The Nashville Palace bar and restaurant, TP's favorite watering hole where he spends a lot of his time when he's in Nashville. Through the years the two have shared many adventures, both at the Palace and on the road.

TP has met many celebrities at the Palace and through his friendship with Hobbs. One of those celebrities is Hobbs' friend, former Los Angeles Dodger's manager and Baseball Hall of Fame member Tommy Lasorda.

Hobbs recalls "one of those special moments" in his relationship with TP that showed just how far these two friends had come from their humble beginnings. "Tom and I were sitting in the Palace one night when we got word that Tommy Lasorda, who was staying at the Opryland Hotel across the street, was ready to be picked up. I was supposed to take him someplace and I asked Tom to come along with me."

As they were sitting in the car waiting for Lasorda to come out, Hobbs looked over at TP and made a point. "Tom," Hobbs said, "Would you have dreamed 20 years ago that you and I would be sitting over here in a big new car, each with a little money in our pocket, waiting for Tommy Lasorda to get in the car with us?"

Think Tom, Think!

Any person who knows TP, knows the guy has a remarkable memory. However, on one outing with Lasorda and Hobbs, it failed him.

Hobbs and TP were in St. Louis with Lasorda, Steve Yeager the catcher, and a bunch of the other ball players. After drinking for awhile, Tom was quite high but that didn't keep him from realizing he should be taking pictures. He went upstairs, got his camera, rejoined the group and proceeded to take two rolls of film of the group.

A few hours later, he bid the group adieu and went upstairs to bed, leaving his camera on the table. Hobbs saw it and took it back to his own room for the night. The next morning TP goes down to breakfast and joins Hobbs in the restaurant. They start talking about the previous night and Tom says he should have gotten some photos of the group.

"Tom can usually remember just about anything, even when he has been drinking heavily, but this time, something happened," Hobbs said. "It's the only time I ever saw that happen to him." Hobbs played along for awhile before handing over the camera and telling TP that in fact, he did take photos the night before, two rolls of them!

John Hobbs, left, and TP visit with baseball legend Stan (The Man) Musial.

16

KNOWING MINNESOTA FATS

An international celebrity named Rudolph Wanderone Jr., better known by most as Minnesota Fats, lived his last years in Nashville and was a regular at Johnny Hobbs' Nashville Palace.

Thanks to TP, Fats got to meet many of the carnival, fair and park people who visited the Palace. He came in to eat, but never drank or smoked, which TP says distinguished him totally from the other patrons. During many year, Fats, thanks to his blustering personality, was the most recognizable name in the history of pool. In addition to being a great pool player, he was a comic and a showman.

TP got to shoot with Fats once, but it was a game of bumper pool, not real pool, the game in which Fats excelled. Hobbs gave TP a $100 bill to help persuade Fats to play a game with him and to the surprise of all, he accepted. It was probably the biggest crowd ever to watch a game of bumper pool at the Palace. TP won.

When his friends would come to the Palace, TP took great pride in introducing them to Fats. "It was amazing to see some of these people's starstruck reaction on meeting the great Minnesota Fats. He was always so cordial and he would always agree to have his picture taken with whoever wanted one," said TP.

Country singer John Michael Montgomery was performing at the Palace one night and TP suggested he meet Fats. "John Michael was thrilled. He had a big smile and he kept shaking hands with Fats. I took a picture of the two and ran it in the paper."

TP thinks he must have taken at least a hundred pictures of Fats. People just wanted to have their picture made with Minnesota Fats, and if they asked for his autograph he had a stamp. He stamped it. As Fats got older, he got feeble and it was practically impossible to carry on a conversation with him.

The last picture TP took of the 90-something year old Fats was at the Christmas party at former Nashville-based carnival owner Ed Gregory's house. For once in his life, Fats had to share equal billing that night, as another one of the guests was pretty famous himself, 88-year old Gene Autry.

While he's never been to Fat's grave, Tom was told by Teresa Bell, Fat's widow, that the epitaph reads: Beat everybody living on earth. Now, St. Peter, rack 'em up."

Jeff Davis, TP, Lib Hatcher, and Randy Travis.

17

TP MEETS THE STARS

Living in Music City USA has given TP the opportunity to meet many country entertainers and traveling for *Amusement Business* has given him equal opportunities across the country.

If there were one single place where TP has met the most celebrities, it would have to be John Hobbs' Nashville Palace. "You can't go anywhere where Tom doesn't know somebody on stage, and they all know Tom," said Hobbs. "A lot of the Grand Ole Opry stars performed at the Palace over the years and Tom got to know most of them."

Always the journalist, even at 2 a.m. on a Saturday under the influence and in a bar in his own town, TP has his notepad and camera always ready. If he sees a booking agent, an entertainer, or even a park owner or carnival worker, he corners them for a story and photo.

"I remember late one night Dale Morris, who headed up the group Alabama came in and within an hour, TP had Dale sitting down over in a corner doing a story, each with a drink in hand," Hobbs recalls.

Sitting in his usual seat one Tuesday night, TP told Hobbs that he was short one photo for the fairs section of the paper and that he had to have one by mid-day Wednesday to fill the space on the page. After crying in several Scotch and waters, someone came up and tapped him on the back and said, "Aren't you Tom Powell?" It was Hardy Huntley, manager of the Pinellas County (Fla.) Fair and his wife Janet. Tom smiled, confirmed that it was indeed him, went out to his car and got his camera, came back in and got the fair photo he needed. "That kind of stuff happens to him all the time," Hobbs said. "He just sits there and the world comes to him."

Finding Randy Travis

TP was the first Nashville journalist to take pictures of Randy Travis way back when he was a cook and dishwasher at the Palace. TP started taking pictures of him with other celebrities and they would be published in AB. Hobbs thinks to this day that TP's early pictures and stories about Travis, whose real name is Randy Traywick, helped him achieve super stardom.

"Every time I would take a picture of somebody at the Palace, Lib Hatcher, who was then manager of both the Palace and of Randy's career and who is now Randy's wife, would bring him out of the kitchen and put him in the photo." Ronny Robins, Marty's son, once asked TP how Travis got his picture in AB so much. TP told him to get to know Lib Hatcher.

Among the entertainers he has met at the Palace are Alan Jackson, Ricky Van Shelton, and Lorrie Morgan. "He knew them before they were stars. They would come into the Palace to hang out because this is where the Opry stars hang out. Alan used to come in every night about nine and stay until one in the morning and sing on the stage whenever he got the chance. Tom got to know all kinds of people before they ever had a hit and wrote stories about them and took their pictures," Hobbs notes.

In addition to meeting a lot of the Grand Ole Opry stars at the Palace, TP spent a lot of time backstage at the Opry. It was not unusual for him to meet his friends at the Palace and take them across the street to the Opry House. He would get them backstage and walk them around introducing them to many of the stars. Once he got them settled into the seats on the stage wings, he would usually leave and go back to the Palace.

When friends would call TP for free Opry tickets, he usually said he would go one step further, he would get them backstage. In reality, it was a lot easier to get them back stage than get free tickets for out front, thanks to the generosity of Jerry Strobel who was then manager of the Grand Ole Opry house.

TP originally met Marty Robbins at the Palace but saw him a lot back stage and over time, they became good friends. In addition to his musical prowess, Robbins was driving racecars when TP was covering the races at the Nashville Speedway for *The Tennessean*. "He always told me that the one thing he wanted that he never got was Entertainer of the Year and he really deserved it because he was a true entertainer. "He told me he never took more than $12,500 for a date because he wanted everybody to make money. At that time he could have been getting $25,000 or $30,000."

A Diamond Of An Entertainer

Tommy Collins, who booked the Tour of Champions On Ice show also was Neil Diamond's concert merchandise man for years. Collins told TP that Diamond, one of TP's favorite entertainers, never gets on a plane without an AB to read. At a Diamond concert in Florida, Collins met TP outside the venue with t-shirts, tickets and earplugs. TP took the shirts and tickets but handed the earplugs back to Collins. "No thanks, I want to hear him," TP said.

After the show, he went backstage and met Diamond who told him that "AB is one of the two publications I read from cover to cover every week. I love to read about those fairs and carnivals." He never did tell Tom what the other publication was that he read regularly.

Another TP favorite, Tom Jones, came to Nashville for a concert during the summer of 1980, promoted by Nashville promoter Lon Varnell. TP was invited to the show and an after-concert party. He took along a couple of co-workers and they all ended up in the last row in the house. "Lon put us in the lousiest seat in Municipal Auditorium and I'd done a million favors for him. After the show, we go down to the party and they tell us we can't go in, we're not on the list. I'm kissing everybody's ass to get in the party and finally Lon comes by and says, 'Hey Tom, come on in.'

"I thought, yeah, but why in the hell didn't you leave my name here. So I proceeded to drink as fast and as much as I could. They came looking for me and said there was to be a presentation made to Tom Jones for a record going to #1 on Billboard. Since I was the only one there from Billboard (AB's sister publication), they assumed I should do it. I think what a joke this is. I had to kiss everybody's ass to get in here and I'm now going to make the main presentation. I still see it as a bit ironic."

Tom was introduced to Jones before the presentation and they talked for awhile. "We were both drinking and he was smoking a cigar. Both our drinks spilled over and everybody started laughing and the presentation went on as planned," TP recalls.

A Rockin' Rodeo

One of TP's favorite stops on his varied travels has been the Houston (Texas) Livestock Show and Rodeo, the second largest exposition in North America. Because of its size and scope, fair managers from across the country make it a point to visit the experience and learn from the event.
It is held in the buildings and parking lots of the Reliant Field complex, which was built adjacent to the Astrodome and all its outbuildings.

Ray Cammack Shows, one of the top carnivals in the country provides the midway. The rodeo is second in prestige and purse only to the National Finals, and there are more than 20 top name concerts during the two-week run. This is heaven for an AB reporter. There are literally hundreds of story opportunities waiting for ink.

While visiting the rodeo in 1982, TP was invited backstage by promoter Lon Varnell to meet Lawrence Welk who had just presented a concert with his orchestra in the giant Astrodome. TP chatted with Welk about the end of his long-running TV show. "It affected me to the extent I practically wanted to change my mind (about giving up the show). It's been a long time since 1903 (his birth year) and its time for me to quit," Welk said. TP asked him if he would miss performing once he retired from the road. "I don't think so. I'm basically a farmer. I don't think I'll miss the road too much."

Excuse Me, Mr. Buffett

In 1983, TP and Thaxter Trafton were backstage at the Nashville Fairgrounds during the MCA Record Label Show during the annual country music fan celebration Fan Fair, now known as the Country Music Association Music Festival.

Earlier in the day, TP had arranged to interview the man who was handling the lights and sound for the concerts. Several hours later when he was ready to do the story, TP thought he saw the guy backstage, went up to him and noticed that he had changed shirts.

The man was sitting on a retaining wall, drinking a beer and chatting with friends. TP walked up, said "Hi" and commented about the guy changing into a brightly colored Hawaiian shirt. "No, I haven't changed shirts," the guy said, obviously surprised by the question. "Aren't you the sound and light man?" TP queried. "No, I'm not," the man laughed. "I'm Jimmy Buffett."

As TP slunk away, he couldn't believe he had not recognized Buffett, whose concert was about to begin. Humbly, TP recalls. "You can imagine my chagrin. Here was not only an outstanding artist, but a guy who broke into the music business while working for *Amusement Business* and Billboard." Buffett worked at the magazines in various capacities, including the mailroom, in 1969 and 1970.

In 1985, TP became even more famous when he officially made it into the *Guinness Book of World Records*, he and 34,999 others that is. They received that distinction when they formed the world's largest kazoo band during halftime of a Vanderbilt University football game in Nashville. The Oak Ridge Boys were on hand to accompany the 35,000 other "musicians" in playing their big hit, Elvira.

The Stars Are Near

Buddy Lee, the late owner of Buddy Lee Attractions, a dominant country music booking agency in Nashville, held great parties at his office and at his home and TP was always invited. Tom met many celebrities during his years as Lee's best friend, including Willie Nelson, Hank Williams Jr. and Garth Brooks.

At Lee's 1989 Christmas Party, TP met Polka King Jimmy Sturr, a multi-Grammy award-winning musician. "Proving what a small world this really is, I found out that night that Jimmy and I both graduated from the University of Scranton, not the same year, of course," TP recalls. "And he's not Polish, he's Irish!"

One of TP's favorite stories about entertainers is about the Jerry Lee Lewis concert he attended in 1996 at Nashville's historic Ryman Auditorium. Lewis had TP and the rest of the audience on their feet rockin' and rollin' during more than 90-minutes of red-hot, rip-roaring rollicking entertainment. "At one point," TP recalls, "Somebody in the audience shouted out for him to play Great Balls of Fire. Without missing a beat, Jerry Lee answered. 'Son, I haven't missed doing it at a show for the last 40 years. I don't intend to start tonight.'"

Access to the stars doesn't always come easy. Tom had arranged to take a picture of the Dixie Chicks while they were at the Kentucky State Fair in Louisville in 2000. He showed up at the prescribed time, but was told the girls weren't ready and that he had to wait.

Concessionaire Stan Minker had driven Tom and Christine over to the stage area on a golf cart, excited that he too would get a chance to meet the act. Stan and Christine left when they found they would have to wait but Tom decided to wait it out, a wait that turned out to be more than an hour.

"Christine and I went back to my air-conditioned office. I wasn't going to wait for anybody, even the Dixie Chicks in that kind of heat. Christine and I returned, all rested and cooled down about an hour and 15 minutes later. We found Tom, all sweaty, sitting on a bench outside the dressing rooms. But he was happy because he got his pictures."

One of the first acts TP met in Nashville was Danny Davis, the leader of the Nashville Brass. Davis played a lot of fairs in the 1980s and 1990s, and TP seemed to see Davis everywhere he went. In 2000, TP and Christine were in a hotel in Tampa while attending the annual carnival convention in nearby Gibsonton. Davis was staying in the same hotel while in town to play a concert at the Florida State Fair.

"Tom ran into me in the lobby one evening and out of the blue, he asked me to get my trumpet and come to his room, without telling me what it was all about," said Davis. "I think the world of Tom, so of course, I did as he requested. I went down to his room and he says 'today is Johnny Hobbs birthday.'" Hobbs is a mutual friend of both.

TP wanted Davis to call Hobbs and "he wanted me to play Happy Birthday for him. I think the both of us yelled into the phone: 'This is just for you, John' and I played Happy Birthday and at the end I played a clam (a distorted shrill note) purposely. "Hobbs was thrilled."

The Silver Screen

Always the first to enjoy a good laugh, TP describes his meeting with cartoonists Bill Hanna and Joe Barbera, "as a genuine thrill." The team of Hanna Barbera created The Flintstones, Yogi Bear, and Top Cat, among others. "They have made me laugh a lot during my days. It was an honor to meet them and thank them for those laughs," TP admits.

Another star of the silver screen, Gene Autry, was a boyhood idol of Tom's. Autry visited Nashville for a board meeting of the National Cowboy Hall of Fame in March 1983 and Tom was invited to the press conference, an invitation he didn't hesitate in accepting. Following the official gathering, TP talked a little baseball with Autry, then owner of the California Angels. "He was most gracious in posing for pictures and signing autographs for the many who requested them. It was a big day for me to meet him."

TP and Christine had the opportunity to visit with another singing cowboy in spring 1995 when they had lunch with the legendary Roy Rogers and Dale Evans at the Roy Rogers Museum in Victorville, Calif. Ed and Jo Gregory of United Shows of America who were good friends with the Rogers, arranged the meeting.

Later during that same visit to California, Tom and Christine attended a California Angels baseball game in Anaheim Stadium and were escorted to the suite of the team's owner, Gene Autry. TP got to talk with him again and take a few photos, again thanks to Gregory.

A Different Kind Of Music

The performing arts have never been an important part of TP's life, although he enjoys a good play or musical when he gets the chance. In June 1981 while attending the play "Best Little Whorehouse in Texas" at the new Tennessee Performing Arts Center in Nashville, TP ran into country male vocalist of the year, Jack Greene in the lobby during intermission and they talked about the show.

Knowing that Greene had played in Texas a great deal both as a singles act and for five years as a member of the Ernest Tubb's band, TP asked Greene how many times he had visited the Chicken Ranch, the house of ill repute that served as the setting for the play they were watching. Greene laughed and said he had heard of it "of course," but had never been there.

The following week, at the same venue at a gala thrown by MCA Records, the Oak Ridge Boys played their first major concert in Nashville. TP observed that the performance was a good indication that musical concerts fit in well as part of the performing arts. "It introduced a whole new audience to the beautiful new performing arts center, a crowd that probably never would have gone there to see a play," TP said.

Growing With Loretta

In his early days in Nashville, when he held down several jobs at the same time and before he joined *Amusement Business,* TP worked part-time for Bruce Lehrke, who then owned Loretta Lynn's Longhorn Rodeo and was involved with the International Rodeo Association's publication, *Rodeo News.* TP became editor for the magazine and conducted publicity chores for the rodeo.

During the summer of 1969, Loretta Lynn's Longhorn Rodeo was booked every Friday, Saturday and Sunday for the entire summer in the same arena in Nashville. "If Loretta's rise to fame and fortune depended on those rodeo dates, she'd be back in Butcher Hollow, Ky.," TP remembers. "To say attendance was dismal is putting it mildly."

But he did have plenty of time to get to know Loretta. "There were some Sundays that I felt as though Loretta was singing just for me," he laughs, admitting that the thing he misses most about those days was the $100 a week.

18

TP & BUDDY LEE

The late Buddy Lee was a former professional wrestler and wrestling promoter when he began booking talent out of Nashville at the Buddy Lee Company, now considered a legendary name in country music.

TP and Lee became fast friends once they met. TP got invited to all the famous Buddy Lee parties that were frequented by Lee's acts, including Ed Ames, Hank Williams Jr., and Willie Nelson. Lee had met Tom when he moved to Nashville from Columbia, South Carolina. Lee and Audrey Williams, Hank Williams widow, set up an agency originally to book Hank Williams Jr. when he was 12 years old. That's how Buddy Lee Attractions was born.

Buddy Lee booked talent into a great many fairs. In the earlier days, TP would go with Lee to some of those fair dates to get stories and photos. One

Buddy Lee, left, actor Joseph Campanella, and TP.

year, Lee had several acts booked at the DuQuoin (Ill.) Fair and he suggested that TP and AB's sales director Ray Pilszak go with him. They were going to drive there in Lee's motor home and they weren't going to leave until after midnight because of prior commitments.

Prior to departure, TP went out with friends in Nashville and drank until being picked up in the motor home by Lee and Pilszak. "They picked me up and before we got out of town Buddy told Ray he was going to pull a trick on me. I was in the back sleeping and the way Buddy was driving, I thought we'd been in a wreck. I rolled off the bed and thought I was going to die."

Early Morning at The Fair

They arrived safely in DuQuoin around 6 a.m. on Sunday and went into a restaurant for breakfast. Lee says to the waitress "What have you got on your menu?" He was talking like a mobster and the waitress said something and Lee says to her, "you're laughing at me aren't you," and she says, "no, sir, I'm not laughing." "He loves joking with people like that and because of his size and because he was an ex-wrestler, few people ever challenged his humor," adds TP.

Norb Bartosik was the manager of the fair at that time and this being a Sunday morning, a religious service was taking place on the fairgrounds in one of the large tents. Lee was driving TP and Pilszak around on a golf cart, with TP sitting in the back looking straight out backward. Lee takes the golf cart and backs it up to the front with TP facing the preacher. "It was like he was preaching directly to me. And I'm saying to Buddy, will you move this thing, and he's saying show some respect," recalls TP.

Lee then decided to go the hotel for awhile and told TP he would catch up with him a little later, which turned out to be about 12 hours later. Luckily there was racetrack action going on that afternoon and Pilszak and TP ended up spending most of their day betting the races.

To help get TP to come along to the fair with him, Lee had promised an interview with Willie Nelson that night. Lee took TP out back to Willie's bus. Willie looks at TP and says "This man looks like he could use a cold beer." Tom got his cold beer and that was the night he met Willie for the first time. Following the official interview, TP looked at Willie and said, "I've got to ask you one more question."

Tom said to Willie "We are the same age, what is it with the bandanna and beard, when will you drop all of that?" Willie smiled and replied: "I tried it with the coat and tie and it didn't work. As long as my fans appreciate my work, I will keep this look." Tom smiled, Willie smiled, and they became friends.

Following that first meeting with Nelson, TP and Lee would often ride along on the bus with Willie to concerts and they would end up being the in-transit entertainment for the singer. "Willie loves story telling, and when you would put Buddy and Tom together, you got some great stories," Tony Conway, now president of Buddy Lee Attractions said.

"They would spend long hours riding along on the bus laughing, talking and telling stories. Tom would always talk about all these characters he knew in the carnival business and the fun people in the fair business and Buddy would talk about all the people he knew growing up in New York and when he was a wrestler. Willie would just laugh and enjoy himself."

Willie Nelson and TP.

On one of those trips, Willie, who was trying to pay a huge IRS tax bill to the government, told TP that the album that was specifically recorded to raise money to help pay that bill, was selling well. "The IRS did me a favor by giving me all this publicity. I never had an album promoted so well in the past, a helluva lot better than any record company ever did," he told TP.

Finding the Fight

One night Lee and TP wanted to see the Sugar Ray Leonard-Leland fight but couldn't find a place that had it on television. They called John Hobbs and he told them he thought he could get it at the Palace. By the time Lee and TP drank a few rounds at Lee's office that afternoon and got to the Palace, Hobbs had already gone but left word for Lee to eat what he wanted. He ate about seven full orders of chicken wings. This was typical for him, according to TP.

The fight was not on at the Palace, but Hobbs could pick it up at his house, so he called and invited Lee and TP over, both of whom were already several sheets to the wind. After the fight, Hobbs who was the only sober one in the group, suggested he drive Lee, who lived way out in the country, home. TP rode along.

When they arrived at Lee's house, the true comedy of errors began. A dog ran up and scared TP who doesn't like dogs, and the 400-pound Lee fell down. Hobbs and TP had a hard time getting Lee back on his feet and up the steps to the house.

Lee went in, woke up his wife Rita and had her open the bar and cook the guys a meal. Meanwhile, Lee went to bed, leaving TP and Hobbs waiting for Rita to cook a meal they really didn't want. After eating and drinking a bit more, the two left the house only to be confronted by the dog that was camped out by Hobbs' car. Hobbs ran to the car and yelled to TP that it "was every man for himself!"

Lee's Open Bar Policy

Lee's Music Row office was an after-work watering hole for many in the industry, including TP. Tony Conway, now president of Buddy Lee Attractions, recalls that he was often sent out to buy more Scotch because Lee had gotten word that TP was on his way over.

"It was kind of like a bar, an after-work (and often after-hours) place to hang out. They would just talk and drink and have a good time all night, and they would often stay here until 2 or 3 in the morning," Conway said.

Printed here for the first time anywhere is a fact few people know about TP. He loves to sing, or at least he loved to sing duets with Buddy Lee. "TP liked to sing when he was with Buddy and they would start doing singing duets," Conway said. "It was amazing, they would just be talking about something and all of a sudden they'd say let's do "Tiny Bubbles."

Lee would call Tom at home at 2 or 3 in the morning to wake him up and he would start pleading with Tom to please sing "Tiny Bubbles." "So you can imagine being woken up at that hour in the morning and have to sing on the phone to keep your friend happy. Buddy loved doing that to TP and Buddy would laugh so hard just telling me about it the next morning," Conway remembers.

Buddy Lee was a millionaire and owned many houses in Nashville, one of which he let TP live in after his divorce. Knowing where to find him, Lee, who was a notorious night person, knocked on TP's door late on many of night. TP was working at AB at that time and needed to be in the office the next morning. Lee could sleep until noon if he wanted. TP would plea with him, but would usually end up going out for a few drinks or they would go to a coffee shop or a truck stop and just sit and talk.

During those late nights, they often drove around and would go into all-night grocery stores or convenience stores where Lee would move the albums of the acts that he was working with to the front of the racks. "I enjoyed being with him. He was fun and we were treated like royalty wherever we went because of who he was," said TP.

19

THE AIRPORT CONNECTION

Flying as often as TP does not only leads him to interesting destinations, but it also gives him a lot of frequent flyer miles which he most often uses for upgrades to First Class when possible. In true TP fashion, flying up front has opened many interesting doors for him.

One celebrity he met while flying in First Class was Tip O'Neill when he was speaker of the house. "We were both in First Class and after we landed, it took about 10 minutes for them to get the door open. We were standing there and started up a conversation."

O'Neill had several bags and TP only had one, so he offered to help the speaker with one and he accepted the help. "As we stood there and as we walked out, I did a mini-interview with him and one thing I asked him was what park he visited the most as he was growing up. He said Paragon Park, in Hull, Massachusetts. I then asked him what his favorite group was and he said Alabama.

"As luck would have it, Dale Morris, the manager of Alabama was on the same flight and I pointed him out to Tip and asked if I could get a photo of the two. He said yes and Dale Morris was thrilled."

Another chance meeting on a plane landed TP an autograph from Roger Staubach, his son Kevin's favorite football player. "I was sitting on the plane when he walked in I said, hey, Roger and he says, 'hey.' After we got off the plane, I started thinking I should have asked him for an autograph for Kevin, but it was too late. So I go into the bathroom, look up and guess who's standing next to me, Roger Staubach. I said I know this is a strange time to ask you this but when we get finished here would you mind autographing something for my son. He laughed and he said okay. After we washed our hands, he gave me his autograph."

In July 1993 while standing in line to board a plane out of Nashville, Tom found himself standing behind rock legend Ted Nugent who had played a concert in town the night before at the Starwood Amphitheater in front of 11,000 fans. TP introduced himself and Nugent offered back that he too was an editor, of *The World Bowhunter Magazine*. They talked for awhile as the line moved slowly forward and Nugent started talking about country music and about being in Nashville.

"We're just like country, only louder," he said of his rock band. "I look like Garth Brooks, but he has puffier cheeks than me...and I bet I can outshoot (with bow and arrow) any country artist." What surprised Tom was how they parted. "He looked at me, shook my hand and said 'thanks for saying hello.' I wonder how many other rock stars would have done that?"

John A. Hobbs, Gene Autry, TP and John C. Hobbs.

20

SCOTCH & WATER, PLEASE

"Powell is a throwback to the days of razzle-dazzle, hard drinking, tough-talking journalism. Under his guidance and by his examples, *Amusement Business* has evolved into one of the most readable trade papers in the industry. His "TP on AB" weekly columns are gems of show business observations, as well as a guide to the best watering holes and hardiest drinking buddies in the Western Hemisphere."

That's the way he was described in the 1987 edition of "In Charge: Music Row's Decision Makers," written by Ed Morris, a former Billboard writer. TP laughs at that assessment of himself and says that's the first time he and Ed had ever agreed on anything.

Tom drinks hard, he plays hard and neither seems to interfere with his journalistic abilities. He can get more done with 8 or 10 Scotches in him than most reporters can while stone sober.

Attraction owner Dennis Carollo said TP's drinking and his legendary status are good for the publication. "He's got such a pipeline with these people. He can sit at one stool at Gibtown (short for Gibsonton, Fla., site of the largest carnival trade show in the world) for two days and get 40 stories done. Everybody has a story and they know where he is, and they come over and he gets all his stuff."

> **TP ON TP**
>
> *"An optimist sees the glass as half full. A pessimist sees it as half empty. A realist sees it as one more thing to wash. I'm a realist and when I see my glass half full, I figure it's time to order two more Scotch and waters."*
>
> *- Tom Powell*

If TP were staking his claim today, his notoriety as a hard drinker could very well be detrimental to his reputation as well as the publication. But it certainly didn't hurt his climb to the top during his era.

Everybody Loves Somebody

Dick Geyer of the Wisconsin Center District, sees TP as the Dean Martin of this industry. "Tom drank, he partied, he worked hard and he was the best out there. Why would anybody condemn someone like that, especially during those days?" Geyer said TP's legendary drinking prowess was played up, as was Dean Martin's, and the industry embraced it and still has fun with it.

During a convention in Phoenix in 1986, Geyer got a call from TP that he was on his way from the airport. "I told him I'd have the Scotch and water ready for him and he says just make sure there is plenty of Scotch." Upon arrival, TP got out of the car and rushed right to the bathroom. Geyer had the bartender mix a couple of Scotch and waters and he took them into the bathroom on a tray while he was standing at the urinal. "You should have heard him laugh," Geyer recalls.

Knowing of his love for Scotch and his ability to consume great quantities at a time, his friends at one function had a surprise for him when he joined them at the bar. There in front of TP were two buckets and a glass. In one bucket was Scotch and water, already mixed, the other bucket had ice. When he finished one drink, he would dip his glass into the bucket, fill it up, throw in some ice, and get on with his drinking, with no need to wait for the waitress to show up.

TP loves to drink, but he also loves good conversation and the two go together well for him in most situations. Former building manager and long time TP friend, Bill Luther, remembers the night he, TP and a full bottle of Scotch sat down in front of a televised World Series baseball game. "I got up to leave several hours later and the bottle was empty and I know I hadn't drunk that much," Luther remembers. "What made it so amazing is that he was in better shape than I was."

One night, he and friends George Smith and Don Sandefur were to go out for dinner in Minneapolis at one of TP's favorite restaurants, Ruth's Chris Steakhouse. "We got there early and went into the bar and ran into Denzil Skinner. We started talking and drinking and totally lost track of time. At 11, the waitress came up and said the kitchen would be closing in a few minutes so if we wanted to have dinner, we'd better hurry. By that time we were both floating but we were hungry so we ate. When we got up to leave, I couldn't walk straight for hours, but you know, that Scotch didn't seem to affect him at all. In all our years, I never saw him out of control."

Friends in Bar Places

It only makes sense that TP's closest friend in Nashville would be a bar owner, John Hobbs. And who better to speak of TP's drinking than the owner of the Nashville Palace, a popular Music City bar and restaurant.

There's a painting of TP on the ceiling of the Palace, and he's the only customer there with his personal chair and a perpetual "Reserved for Tom Powell" sign on the table. John Hobbs said Tom gets upset when someone is sitting in his chair. "Sometimes a tourist comes in, moves the sign and sits down in his seat. Tom comes up to me and says 'What the hell are they doing in my chair?' He doesn't want to drink anywhere but that one chair. That's his seat and nobody else's. He'll ask them to move, just like Norm does on the television show "Cheers," Hobbs said.

TP hired Ray Waddell as a reporter for AB in the late 1980s. "A lot has been said about Tom's prodigious drinking, but I'll say this: he has never, ever let drinking get in the way of his job. In fact, if anything it has enhanced his ability to do his job. I've never seen him stagger or act anything less than professional. He just might laugh a little louder and become a bit more friendly," says Waddell, who is now senior editor of *Billboard*, based in Nashville.

Waddell said he likes Tom's style. "TP appreciates and expects hard work, but not at the expense of knocking back a few. While he would never condone drinking at the office, he had no problem if you left the office to interview somebody at a bar, then came back."

"I've owned a club for more than 30 years and I've never seen a man who could drink as much as Tom. We counted one night and he had 56 drinks with an ounce and a quarter in them and was able to walk out. His average is about 30 drinks a night. Thirty drinks is equal to a fifth of Scotch," said Hobbs. "I'm going to put his liver in the Smithsonian Institute because there's got to be something special about his liver."

Duke Smith of Allied Specialty Insurance once said that Tom should donate his liver to the Mayo Clinic because they could learn a great deal from it.

Sporting Booze

TP was in a Nashville bowling league with fellow AB staffers Ray Pilszak and John McCartney. Pilszak, who takes his bowling scores and his team standings a bit more seriously than does Tom, recalls one particular evening.

"We had some time to kill before our game, so we went over to Buddy Lee's and Tom and McCartney started drinking and Tom got sort of blitzed and I got sort of ticked off. I said, Tom, you're going to mess us up and ruin our team. As it turned out Tom bowled his first 600 series. So maybe the booze helped him."

Another alcohol-sports combination also took place in Nashville. Pilszak and TP were on the Buddy Lee-sponsored softball team. They won several championships over the years and TP was not only a player, but also the manager. As usual, the boys were drinking quite a bit before this particular game.

Pilszak picks up the story: "As manager, TP made up the lineup and after having a few drinks he decides he's going to be clean-up batter and play third base. Several balls got by him at third base, so he moved himself to second base and the same thing happened there. He got up to bat two times and struck out both times, something he rarely did. The final blow came when a simple grounder came toward him at second base. He went after it and just kinda rolled over onto the ground. At that point he walks up to me and says 'I better get out of the game.'"

Slowing Down

As any true thoroughbred, TP is slowing down a bit as he ages. "I've watched him slow down. Since the cancer operation he has slowed down a lot. He's not drinking as much and he's not coming out as much. He used to come out every night. Now maybe just three or four nights a week; four is a bonus. In fact, I had to lay off two bartenders when he slowed down on his drinking," John Hobbs laughed.

AB's publisher Karen Oertley, said TP is a tough guy with a high pain threshold. "He's real tough. He had that bout with cancer and the following chemotherapy, and it just didn't seem to knock him off the line one bit. He doesn't feel pain. I think he must have a very high tolerance for pain or discomfort or maybe it's the Scotch. I don't know," she laughed. "I told him he had the wrong calling in life. He should have been a linebacker, because he can keep right on going."

Oertley said she has never been concerned about Tom's drinking being a problem or getting in the way of him doing his job at the paper. "I've seen him feel the effects of a good solid 10 hours of drinking and he is remarkable. I mean it's legendary that Tom can be absolutely plastered the night before and get up early the next morning and seem to feel no effect, which is part of my no pain theory. He remembers all the details when you thought he was just way too far gone to know what was going on. That's a very interesting phenomenon about Tom."

Those Were the Hazy, Crazy Days

One night in his earlier days, Tom left the Nashville Palace and was pretty well intoxicated as he drove off. To get to the highway he had to go through a confusing construction zone full of orange barrels and barriers.

"He got stuck in mud about 18 inches deep. He is sitting in his car and my security guard calls me and says, 'Mr. Hobbs, your buddy is in a ditch down here and we're afraid the cops are going to come and he's drunk.' I said get him out of the car real quick," Hobbs recalls. "They get him out and bring him over to Fiddler's (a hotel Hobbs owned at the time next to the Palace). The cops come up and want to know who was driving. My security guards said they didn't know. The guy went home."

TP remembers calling his son Kevin that night asking him to come to the Fiddler's and take him home. "I called and he started lecturing me and giving me all kinds of hell. I said whoa, I'm the father here and I need your help, come and get me." Kevin did as instructed.

Tom shows up the next morning with Kevin and a tow truck. They get the car out of the mud and TP tells the driver that when he stepped in the deep mud the night before, his new shoes came off and were still under the mud. He pointed in the general direction, half expecting the driver to fish out the shoes.

The wrecker driver looks at Tom and says, "We do cars, we don't do shoes," got in his truck and drove off. The shoes are still in the dirt under the well-traveled Briley Parkway.

Shortly after that incident, TP stopped driving after serious drinking. His wife Christine or other friends are usually more than happy to make sure TP gets home after a night of drinking.

NOT REALLY WAITING FOR YOU TOM

"During an IAAPA convention in Dallas we were staying at the Loew's Anatole and one night around 1 a.m. the fire alarm went off. We got up, got dressed and went down the stairs. I guess it was about 3:30 and we were all still sitting around the lobby and I look up and in walks Tom with some others. He looks at me and says 'What the hell are you doing down here waiting up for me in your pajamas?' I said you're crazy, Tom. As you can imagine, he had been out enjoying himself."

-Bruce McKinney, Hersheypark

TP on Tom's Drinking

Tom thinks the biggest misconception about Tom Powell is that he drinks too much. "A lot of people think I'm an alcoholic, but I'm not. Some of the best stories I've ever reported have come from drinking with people. Some of the best acquaintances have resulted from the same."

People comment all the time that they can't believe TP can drink so much all night long and still be up attending an 8 a.m. meeting. How does he do it? "Easy," he says. "I've always done it and if the job calls for me to be up the next morning, I will be up the next morning because that's what I do. I have fun and I pay the piper when I have to."

The big question is, does Tom drink as much as the legend and the stories would have you believe? "I hardly ever drink at home during the week, only when I go out or am on the road. But when I drink, I drink." Christine agrees with that assessment and believes that most people think Tom drinks a whole lot more than he does. "Believe me, when he is out drinking, he drinks a lot. But when we're at home, he'll usually drink Diet Pepsi. We made it a point to start drinking soft drinks at home several years ago."

The policy of not drinking alcohol at home came as a result of a compromise with his doctor. The doctor said "I know what your lifestyle is when you're on the road and you're not going to change that but when you're home just don't drink." When TP and Christine are both in Nashville on a Saturday, they claim it as their special day and that's when they allow themselves to drink at home. "It's our day to be together."

John Hobbs thinks TP has two different personalities. One when he drinks, the other when he doesn't. He likes the drinking personality the best. "My wife says if TP didn't drink she wouldn't want to be around him. She said he's no fun sober. He doesn't joke and kid as much when he's sober. When he's drinking he's cutting up, kidding, and having a big time. He's really like a Dr. Jekyll and Mr. Hyde. When he's sober he's straight and he doesn't kid a whole lot. He's blunt. If you call him he'll talk business real quick and then just hang up. If he's drinking he'll carry on a 30-minute conversation. Yeah, there's a big difference in him."

Bill Luther kids that the more TP drinks, the better his stories get. "Maybe that's why he is known for his storytelling," Luther notes.

One of Bill Alter's favorite drinking stories about TP took place in Gallagher's Restaurant in New York City. The bar was around the corner from the office of the National Ticket Company, where Alter worked. He, TP and Jack Conway, the president of the company, went to lunch. After a two hour lunch Alter excused himself to go back to the office.

"Three and a half hours later I walked by Gallagher's on my way home only to find they were still sitting on the same stools repeating the same stories they were telling when I left the first time."

The Big Question

Is Tom an alcoholic? Christine: "I would say no, but I'm not sure what really determines an alcoholic. I mean he could go and probably never drink again in his life. If his doctor told him that he couldn't drink anymore for health reasons he would stop. It wouldn't bother him in the least. To me an alcoholic is someone who gets up in the morning craving a drink."

Hobbs has been around a lot of drunks in his life and he insists TP is not one of them. "He gets up in the morning to go to work and if he decides not to drink he won't drink. I don't believe he's an alcoholic. He just loves the feeling of getting high and enjoying himself. He loves to party. Tom enjoys a good party more than anybody I've ever seen."

Protecting his territory at the Nashville Palace.

Christine jokes that sometimes she wants a drink more than Tom does. "He went for a physical the other day and Dr. Mike Calloway said something about the drinking and all that. Tom says, 'Hey, Christine drinks as much as I do."

About her own drinking, Christine says, "I learned to drink in Gibtown with the big boys where you drink or get off the porch."

21

THE DUKE IN TP'S LIFE

Duke Smith, the founder and owner of Allied Specialty Insurance, and Tom were the closest of friends for many years, until Duke's death in 2002. Smith loved to tease Tom and get him going with the simplest comments. They shared many hours together.

Tom was often at Smith's Florida home for parties and special events and they talked nearly every day for years and more often near the end of Smith's life. They loved to talk about sports, Smith the Chicago White Sox; Tom the Philadelphia Phillies and Boston Red Sox.

TP and Smith go back to the early 1970s. Smith had purchased a carnival in 1970 and was still new at it when TP met him in early 1973.

Dave Smith, Duke's son, said it was a natural connection from the beginning. "Dad was a new carnival owner who loved sports and Tom was a new reporter coming from a sports reporting background. They had a very intimate knowledge of sports and they had many other common interests. They enjoyed a good drink and they enjoyed a good sports match. Duke was trying to get notoriety as a carnival person and Tom was trying to get to know the carnival industry better. They seemed to hit it off, and they had a lifelong relationship from that point forward."

Help For a New Carnival Owner

Smith sold his carnival and began the insurance company, which serviced the carnival industry, in 1974. It was an "I'll scratch your back if you scratch mine" relationship and it worked to both of their benefits. But it only worked because they trusted each other. Tom used Smith to get into areas or get to people that he didn't know and Smith used Tom to get press when he needed it to help his growing insurance business.

While Smith loved to drink as much as Tom, he was fascinated with TP's ability to drink and still remember the facts. "Duke was absolutely enamored with the fact that a guy could drink for 12 hours, or however long and at the 12th hour could remember somebody he had met 15 years earlier. Tom could recall the date, the place, the location, and what happened. It would always just blow Duke away."

Smith proved to be a big help in getting TP established within the carnival community. Knowing Duke Smith opened many doors during a time when carnival owners were wary of the press because of all the bad publicity the industry as a whole was getting. Smith often served as a liaison between wary carnival operators and the greenhorn reporter from AB. "Tom Powell, a friend of mine from AB is looking to do a story and would like to talk to you. You can talk to him and trust him and he's a square type of guy, and he's not going to spin your words around."

> **Tim on TP**
>
> "During baseball season, Tom thrives on televised baseball, especially his favorite team the Philadelphia Phillies. On the days when the Phillies are to play an afternoon televised game, TP skips traditional lunch time and "goes to lunch" about 15 minutes before the game is to start. We smile as he leaves the office, knowing exactly where he's headed."
>
> - Tim O'Brien

Visiting Duke

During a visit to Smith's Treasure Island, Fla. office in July 1989, Smith and his two sons David and Dean took TP to lunch at the local yacht club. To Tom's surprise, the luncheon had been organized and the mayor was there to present TP with the keys to the city. "Even though he was a Republican, I was honored," TP notes.

TP and his wife Christine were often guests at Smith's home, sometimes just to visit, other times for a special event. In 1992, the occasion was a costume ball. Smith came as God, in a white flowing satin robe with gold braid, sporting a full beard and toting a Bible. A sign around his neck had the initials G.O.D., and the words, Good Old Duke. TP, by coincidence, dressed as the devil, and Christine as a she-devil.

On another occasion in March 1993, Smith suggested that TP and Christine, along with Bud and Jeanette Gilmore and Dave Smith and his wife Mary Chris, fly to Key West for lunch in Smith's private plane.

That was TP's first visit to Key West and he said he was "flattered" that several people down there said he looked like Key West's favorite son, Ernest Hemmingway. "But the difference is I can write," he kidded his host.

Around the World With Duke

In the fall of 1997, TP and Christine, Duke Smith and his girlfriend Carolyn Patterson, Rene and Judy Peche, and Bud and Jeanette Gilmore went on an around the world cruise hitting ports in China, Singapore, Australia, Thailand, Bali and others. Rest, relaxation and drinking dominated the six weeks they spent on the trip. TP's and Christine's bar bill for the trip came to $1,900. "We could have taken another cruise for the cost of our bar bill alone," laughed TP.

He had been off work only a couple times during his career at AB. The first following his heart attack, then for a short recuperation period following each hip replacement, but never for a long period. The cruise was the first, and only time, TP ever took an extended leave of absence, with no pay.

Allied Specialty Insurance and *Amusement Business* exhibit at most of the same trade shows and TP is at virtually every one. Duke Smith however, wasn't always there, leaving the Allied booth in the hands of David and his crew.

"Whenever I was at a convention and wasn't doing the right thing or wasn't working real hard, I would get a phone call from dad that night in my hotel room," Smith laughs. "Nine out of ten times I knew the source."

Duke Smith and TP.

TP and animal trainer Gunther Gebel-Williams.

22

THE RABBI IN TP'S LIFE

The late Milt Kaufman was an ordained rabbi as well as president and chairman of Gooding's Million Dollar Midway, at one time one of the largest carnivals around.

TP first met Kaufman just months after joining AB, during the 1972 convention of the International Association of Amusement Parks & Attractions (IAAPA). TP says Kaufman "was as gracious of a host then as he was to be over the next quarter of a century."

Kaufman was a character, almost a caricature of himself. He walked around in colorful suits and was always the gentleman. He also said many times that he was proud to claim TP as a friend. Each year, during the annual International Association of Fairs & Exposition (IAFE) trade show in Las Vegas, Kaufman would host a big dinner for the fair managers and associates at the seafood restaurant in the Sands Hotel and Casino.

Tom was always invited to this event and one year he asked his friend Bill Alter if he wanted to join him. Alter said yes, and that's when the fun began. The story picks up as the two of them head to the Sands. "Tom had already had a lot to drink and I told him he wasn't in good enough shape to even cross the street to get to the Sands. He insisted and said he had to go; he could not pass on this important event for his friend Kaufman who wanted AB to cover the dinner," Alter said.

"So I accepted the challenge and truly had to work to get Tom across the street to the Sands. As we walked into the restaurant Tom was literally bouncing off the wall. Of course this was seen by Milt who rose from his seat and made sure we were seated next to each other as he expressed his concern about Tom.

Drinking Himself Sober

"When the waiter appeared Tom ordered the usual Scotch and water, but I got up and got the waiter to the side and told him that no matter what he orders give him plain water. This is exactly what he did for the next two-and-a-half hours. Tom probably had 8 or 10 glasses of water. After dinner we walked back to Bally's and he said to me, 'that is amazing, I have drunk myself sober!' He never realized he was drinking water the entire time."

Stan Minker was the concession manager for Kaufman's carnival and for many years helped arrange dinners for Kaufman and his friends. "Tom always went over and above his job as a reporter," Minker said. "I remember one time at Bally's we were getting ready to eat and Tom's steak arrived at the table and he started eating. Some people came up to the table who Milt was trying to get their business and said to Tom that he needed a picture. Tom didn't have his camera, so he ran upstairs to his room to get it. Tom just left his steak and went up and got his camera, knowing that his job there was to cover the industry not necessarily to enjoy a dinner."

In 1981, TP came to Kaufman's defense after his contract was nullified and all carnivals were shut out of the Milwaukee Summerfest, starting in 1982. The event's board of directors made the decision not to book any carnivals. In his column, TP said he got upset when he heard the news. "The message I get from reading in-between the lines is 'Thank you Milt Kaufman. We've milked you for all the money we can get and now we don't need you anymore,'" TP wrote.

An editorial in a Milwaukee newspaper ticked off TP even more. "Summerfest directors took a major step toward improvement of the festival's site, tone and image when they voted the other day to cancel the troublesome midway operation." Most of the column was dedicated to the issue that seemed to single Kaufman's carnival out as a sore spot of the event. "If I were Milt Kaufman, I would ask what they mean by a troublesome operation," Tom wrote. "I would make them prove the show was a problem."

Rabbi Kaufman gave the invocation at the closing banquet of the 1988 IAFE. He drew much praise for his non-sectarian remarks. Someone suggested to TP that Clark Robinson, a Mormon, and now president of the IAAPA, should be allowed to give a rebuttal. "While everybody else ate steak, Kaufman enjoyed a specially prepared fruit plate," TP laughs. "He said he was 20 years ahead of time now that everyone is on a health kick and eating fruit."

23

TP MEETS THE PREZ

One of the "biggest thrills of my life" was meeting President Bill Clinton at the White House, TP said. "I'll never forget just standing right next to him and the band is playing "Hail To The Chief" and I heard it announced that ladies and gentlemen, the President...I mean, God, if you don't get shivers on that there's something wrong with you."

> **TP ON TP**
>
> *"Truman and Kennedy have been the best U.S. Presidents ever. The worst has been any Republican."*
>
> *- Tom Powell*

Former carnival owner Ed Gregory had his United Shows of America set up on the White House lawn, and Gregory invited TP and Christine to Washington D.C. Christine found an old button that said "Clinton For Governor," and TP took that along to wear in case he got to meet the President.

They were visiting with Gregory when the word came that the President

TP and President Bill Clinton.

was on his way down to the midway. Everyone lined up to greet him and TP slipped the metal button onto his jacket. "When he got to me he looked at it and asked 'where did you get that?' and we must have talked for 20 minutes. I said my friend, Neil Regan, an undertaker from Scranton buried Hillary's father. Her parents were from Scranton. And he says, 'Oh, we love Scranton, we go up there as often as we can.'"

TP couldn't believe how personable Clinton was and how much time he spent with him. "He got up on stage and he sang with Jim Ed Brown. He did the pop-a-top song. He was great. He was not only great with me but he took time to talk with everybody. It was quite a thrill. Then a curator took all of us on a special tour of the White House."

Close But No Reagan

His only other visit to the White House took place in 1983 when he was there as a member of the Nashville press corps covering a reception being held by President Ronald Reagan for the Country Music Association. The occasion took place the night before a 90-minute TV taping at Constitution Hall to celebrate the 25th anniversary of the CMA. TP enjoyed the experience but didn't come close to getting to meet the President.

Along with Tom at the White House that day, all hoping to shake the President's hands were many of the 48 country music entertainers that were set to be on the following night's show. While waiting for the President to enter the room, TP mingled with the likes of Roy Acuff, Minnie Pearl, Peewee King, Gene Autry, Grandpa Jones, Loretta Lynn, and Tammy Wynette.

Myles Johnson, fair manager from Spencer, Iowa and member of the CMA board, was probably the most surprised when John Block, Secretary of Agriculture came over and started talking with TP. "John's wife and I were judges for a state fair beauty contest in Illinois, and I met him then. Myles kept bringing that up for years, that I knew the Secretary of Agriculture."

As the group was walking about looking at the various historic portraits on the wall, TP glanced over to Tennessee Ernie Ford who had visited the White House many times, and asked him if he ever took the experience for granted. "No way," said the old pea-picker. "It's always a thrill."

Asked the same question, country crooner Mickey Gilley laughed and said "This reminds me of Disneyland. You just wonder if it's real." Jim Halsey, head of his own talent agency at the time answered TP's question with "Heck, I was thrilled just getting a chance to meet Gene Autry."

24

THE PRIEST IN TP'S LIFE

Being born and raised a Catholic has been extremely important to TP. He says his Catholic upbringing more than anything has given him the ability to know right from wrong. TP graduated from the University of Scranton, a Catholic university run by the Jesuits.

It was only natural that he and the now-retired Carny Priest, Monsignor Robert J. McCarthy become buddies. Father Mac, as he is known, was appointed by the Vatican's Pontifical Commission "for the pastoral care of itinerant people and as the official chaplain of the carnivals in the United States."

Father Mac, the "peripatetic, perspicacious padre," as TP likes to call him, is much different from your basic priest. "I have always had a great feeling of respect and appreciation for priests and the humble life most of them live," TP says. "But I was shocked, as any good Baptist, Church of Christ member, Mormon or Jew would be, the first time I met this man."

It is safe to say, TP points out, that Father Mac is no ordinary priest. He says Mass, officiates at baptisms, burials, hears confessions and is a genuinely good, concerned person who cares about others more than he does himself. "The similarities between him and most other priests I have known over the years ends there," notes TP.

The Unorthodox Priest

One doesn't get much out-and-out preaching from Father Mac. He'd never make it on those television shows where making money, rather than saving souls, seems to be the main object. But despite all the kidding and joking around, he is constantly delivering a message of good will. TP feels that "without question, Father Mac is the greatest public relations man the carnival industry has ever known."

In 1996 TP and a group of others convinced Father Mac that a book should be written about his unusual priestly status. It was established that TP was the most practical person to write it and he did, with all proceeds going to the cloistered Sisters of the Precious Blood Monastery in Watertown, N.Y.

A Strong Bond

Through the years, TP and Father Mac traveled and roomed together, cried together, drank together, prayed together and wandered together on the streets of a small Spanish village early one morning totally lost. They are but two Irishmen loving the same people.

"There's a different relationship between us than in most relationships TP has developed," Father Mac said. "I've been kind of a part of their family. He kind of took me in, it's been almost like a brotherhood in a sense."

The entire Tom Powell clan knows and has a special relationship with the priest. TP's children treat him "like a grandfather" and TP's two sons, Kevin and Tommy are always eager to drive anywhere he wants to go when he visits Nashville. Father Mac laughs when he relates that one day TP's wife Christine half-seriously "told me that she felt a little guilty because she broke Tom and I up."

In 2001 when TP was diagnosed with colon cancer and was scheduled to undergo an operation, he understandably was quite scared. He called Father Mac and asked him to come to Nashville to be with him. "He was afraid that he was going to die and he wanted me there. Christine picked me up and took me back and forth to the hospital, but she left Tom and I alone a great deal and we had some wonderful talks," Father Mac said.

CALL ME DADDY

"He's very close to all his kids and tries to call each one at least once a day. He goes crazy if he can't find one of them, if he doesn't know exactly where they are. I say Thomas they're not two anymore."

- Christine Powell

Hi, I'm Father Mac

When Father Mac first met TP, he was duly impressed that he had been educated by the Jesuits in Scranton. When he joined AB, TP made it a point to befriend Father Mac. "I liked him, but really to me, he was just another newspaper man. I didn't immediately swoon over him or become his groupie as so many did. We built our relationship strongly from the ground up," said Father Mac.

TP's Nashville buddy and bar owner John Hobbs knows Tom's religion means a lot to him. "He's a strong Catholic and he goes to church on a regular basis. To his credit, he always made sure his kids went and that they were raised Catholic. We still go to church a lot together. Tom doesn't miss

Mass. If there's any way possible, he's there."

Fortunately for Tom and the others in the industry who try to get to Mass every week, Father Mac is often around at the larger fairs and events where he'll say Sunday Mass. He has offered hundreds of Masses on midways. In the early days, the girly show tent, the Bingo Hall, or the human oddities tent were often the spot chosen because they were usually the largest tents with the greatest capacity.

When TP is on location with Father Mac, he always wants to be a part of those Masses. "He tells me ahead of time that he wants to be the reader and he always wants an active part and he's upset if somebody else wants to do it. But he would take the book and he'd study before he got up to give his reading. He was always pretty good at it."

Father Mac loves to tell jokes and TP says that although he has heard most of them several times, he still has to laugh at one of the priest's favorites. "It's a cute joke, but his delivery is great," TP recalls. "It's especially funny because he brings himself, as a priest, into the joke."

The priest relates that particular story: "I came upon two small boys grieving over the death of their pet dog and they asked me to perform a burial ceremony. I said I couldn't do it because the dog had no soul. I said I felt sorry for them because they lost their pet, and started walking away. Then I heard one ask what they should do with the $75 they had for the ceremony. I stopped and said, wait a minute boys, why didn't you tell me it was a Catholic dog?"

> **PASS THE PLATE**
>
> "I attended Sunday Mass with Tom in a small church in Elysburg, Pa. and when they passed the basket for the offering, Tom took out his check book and wrote a check for $100. I cautioned him that he would now be considered a major benefactor with that size of a contribution to that small of a church."
>
> - Bill Alter, National Ticket Company

John Hobbs says TP's Catholic demeanor is definitely not an act. "He's honest and he's sincere and I'll tell you what. You could trust Tom Powell with your billfold. You can't say that about a lot of people. But Tom Powell will not take a dime from anybody. He's just as straight as they come."

He's also generous. "Tom's got a heart bigger than gold and you know what, money doesn't mean a thing to him. If he's got it he spends it; if he hasn't got it he just does without. He's generous. When he walks into the Palace he'll often say set the bar up for everyone," said Hobbs.

As a friend of the industry, Father Mac is in demand, but on a priest's salary, he needs the support of his itinerant congregation to travel and to be able to serve them. Most of the time, carnival owners, fair managers or various individuals would bring in the priest to a fair or carnival location for special occasions. Tom was also quite generous to Father Mac. "If he wanted

TP with the two Carny Priests, Father Mac, right, and Father John Vakulskas.

me somewhere, even Nashville, he would pay for the flight, the hotel and make arrangements to pick me up. He has been very generous to me through the years," said the padre.

Father Mac thinks TP's strong faith has a lot to do with his upbringing. "He got his foundation in religion from his mother, and then he was influenced a great deal at the University of Scranton. In those days the priests had a stronger contact with the students and I'm sure that had a lot to do with his beliefs."

Father Mac laughs when he recalls, that on several occasions TP told him that he is personally responsible for the priest's notoriety. "He loves to say he made me famous. He tells that to everybody. And I say it to him too. He once said that I would have been nothing if it hadn't been for him and I kid him by saying, by God, I wouldn't Tom. I wouldn't have been anything. I couldn't have made it on my own." While he might not have actually "made" Father Mac famous, he has certainly helped.

The priest enjoys TP's company and he enjoys meeting people when he's with him. "He has introduced me to some of the greatest people in the world. When he introduces me, he always builds me up something fierce and he gives the greatest speech about what a great guy I am," Father Mac relates.

"Of course being the person I am, I enjoy that too. He might not know these people himself, but by God he's going to introduce me to them. He might not even introduce himself but he'll go up and tell that person that they must meet this man over here. Of course by the time I meet the people, TP has painted me as a king."

25

FUN & TRAVELS WITH FATHER MAC

For many years, Father Mac arranged international group travel for the industry. He would pull together an itinerary, sign others up, and in return, he would get a free trip. He often received more than one freebie and in those cases, TP was usually invited along.

"The thing that drove me crazy is that we usually had to room together because I would end up overbooking and the only place for him to stay would be in my room," Father Mac recalls.

As one can imagine the two of them rooming together in a country where neither knows the language created some funny, as well as some tense times during the years. Father Mac relates one of the funnier experiences the two shared on TP's first European experience in 1980.

"We got lost one night. Well, actually we got lost many times in Europe, but this night we were in Rothenburg, Germany. I had been there before and they knew me at the hotel but they didn't know Tom. It was his first trip. He went out that night with several couples and everybody ended up doing their own thing and kind of ignored Tom, so he came searching for me."

Father Mac had arranged with the owners of the hotel to stay at their home instead of the hotel because he wanted a bit of privacy to get some rest.

"Well, he found me and he got me out of bed, and I ended up going out with him. We're walking around the city and finally came to this nightclub that was packed with people. The two of us stood in the door and at a nearby table was a group of rather attractive ladies. They spotted us and signaled for us to come over and sit with them."

Room For Two More?

TP and the priest joined the ladies. "They couldn't speak English and we couldn't speak German, but we all drank and had a good night of it. We were able to figure out that the ladies were all housewives on a bowling team celebrating a victory of some kind."

In Rothenburg, the street lights were shut off at midnight and when the two came out of the bar, not only did they not know which direction to head, but the streets were totally dark. "We started walking and walking. We were the only ones on the street at that hour in the morning. Tom was good and drunk by then but he said he knew which hotel he was in because there was a dog sitting in front of it when we left," Father Mac laughs.

"We just walked and walked and we actually ended up in front of the hotel, but we weren't sure that it was ours. So, here were the two of us standing out front talking rather loudly. Bill Capell's daughter Barbara was up in her room asleep but she heard the two of us talking and she hollered out the window.

"She said 'is that you, Father?' I said, yes, are we at the right hotel? And she assured me that we were. The first thing we had to do was get the hotel manager out of bed. He had to unlock the doors or we couldn't get in. He let us in at last. It was so late and I was so tired, I just stayed there that night."

The dog that TP had been planning on using as a landmark had moved. The next year, Tom didn't go on the tour but the group went back to the same hotel. He received a postcard signed by everyone saying the dog had died.

Albert and Dennis Carollo, hotel and attraction owners in Michigan greet Father Mac with the proverbial question.

Father Mac, a Big Mac & a Brew

On that same German trip, while the group was in Heidelberg, many in the group, including TP, were impressed that a local McDonald's served beer. Never to pass up a unique drinking opportunity, they all went in. Bill Luehrs, son of carnival owners Hub and Winnie of Luehrs's Ideal Rides, operated a McDonald's franchise in Kansas City and he was especially curious. TP recalls that Bill wanted a picture of himself drinking a beer in front of the menu board. "I snapped one of him, then he snapped one of me."

About that time a girl who had been watching and who TP thought was just another "beautiful and friendly fraulein" approached and offered to take a picture of Bill and TP together. They started a conversation with her by asking where she was from. "Where am I from?" she laughed. "I'm Cindy Hall, Bill's wife. We're from Circus World and we are on the same tour as you!" TP and Bill were duly embarrassed.

Preferring his Scotch on the rocks, TP often got frustrated while in Germany that ice was not readily available, if available at all. At one stop when the hotel had no ice, he walked down to the corner grocery store, asked where the ice was, and a clerk pointed behind the checker. "I couldn't see it myself, so I got in line behind about 40 people and one checker slowly counted up the tabs. "As it became my turn, I asked again where the ice was, and was handed a package. It was ice cream." They had no "real" ice.

A few weeks after returning from that trip, Father Mac wrote a letter addressed to the Employees of *Amusement Business*. It read:

"You fine people who work for AB know Tom Powell for his writing talents, his interest in sports, his bowling ability and many other things, but until you have shared the same bedroom with him, you do not know of his snoring ability. On our recent trip to the Oktoberfest and Germany, I got a total of six hours sleep in the three days we shared the same room in Munich. I never heard anything like it and I can readily see why women love him, and leave him. Other than snoring, Editor Powell is just great! He sings at 3 in the morning and ends up with no less than seven women at the same table in a bar less than 24 hours after reaching a different continent. He was a proud part of the system that forced the Oktoberfest to brew one million extra gallons of beer. Tom became a reader of the scriptures during the trip, which proves that all was not lost, just my sleep."

TP says he doesn't want to accuse a priest of telling lies, but insists he doesn't snore.

Another Country, More Bull

Three years later in Seville, Spain, the two got lost again. "There was a big fair in Seville and the gypsies were there," said Father Mac. "There were about 50 of us on the trip, including Tom and we went to the fair." The hotel keys were big, as they most often are in the older hotels in Europe, and neither TP nor Father Mac wanted to carry them around so they left them at the front desk.

Good idea except they didn't write down the name or the address of the hotel when they headed out to walk around the city one afternoon. "After we had walked for awhile we realized that we were totally lost. We couldn't find someone who spoke English, and of course, neither of us could speak Spanish," Father Mac recalls.

Several hours later they found some people from their tour who had been smart enough to write down the information. The two lost travelers copied it down, flagged down a taxi and headed to the hotel. The next day they didn't get lost, but they ended up somewhere TP didn't particularly like. "I like bull fighting and Tom didn't know anything about it but he would go anyplace I'd suggest, so we went to the bull fight," said the priest, noting that he "forgot" to tell Tom one important fact.

"When you get into the bullfight you can't get out and you've got to stay all day because they don't have an easy way to exit. They don't have aisles or anything. The bullring is a round ring. We got in there and we sat down. The bulls started and my God they have six bulls and the entire program lasts about six hours. Tom had to take a leak and he wanted a drink and he got a bit anxious. He says never again will he ever, ever go to a bullfight."

26

TP'S EUROPEAN ADVENTURES

Father Mac wasn't the only one to share in TP's international adventures. In mid-January 1984, TP and then publisher Howard Lander traveled to Hamburg, Germany for Interschau; the tradeshow for German carnival owners and operators.

It was the newspaper's first trip to this popular trade gathering. Ride broker Dan Glosser, who was selling for German ride builder Zierer at the time and a veteran of these events, helped Tom and Lander set up an after-convention tour to the manufacturing facilities of several European ride builders.

The plan was to attend Interschau, visit the factories, fly to California to catch Super Bowl, and then fly back to Nashville. Dan was helpful in setting up an itinerary that included interviews with some of the biggest ride builders in the world, including Zierer, Intamin, Huss, Zamperla, and Schwarzkopf.

Thanks For The Itinerary, Dan

"We made a big thing out of us going to the show, we were real excited and thought it would be good for AB for us to be there," Lander said. "We arrived in Germany and were very tired, but we wanted to partake in the fun so we decided to go out and ended up not getting back to the hotel until 6 a.m."

As they headed to the elevator to go to their rooms for a brief rest before heading to the trade show, Tom looked up and saw American showman Ron Burback sitting in the lobby. TP had seen him the night before and had set up an interview with him for later in the morning, but he was several hours early. Tom being always the gentleman, told Ron he would be right back down. He went up to his room, quickly showered and got dressed and went back down and did the interview.

Lander was amazed how much Tom could play and still get so much work done, even six time zones away from home. "This guy stayed out drinking till 4 a.m., would come back to his room, take a shower and two aspirins, a quick nap and be back at work at 7 a.m. and drinking again at noon. I just never saw anything like it." But the trade show was to be only the beginning of this European party.

As a veteran European traveler and friend of AB, Dan Glosser had made all the travel arrangements, but he didn't visit all the factories with the AB team. That allowed Tom and Lander to talk openly with the heads of the various companies without having a representative of Zierer, their competitor, in the room.

While not quite the same as the Griswold family's "European Vacation" scenario, the three experienced quite a few bumps in the road. They all admit the situations are much funnier looking back then they were at the time.

Glosser recalls: "We had some really hysterical experiences on that trip. When we got to Zurich we go to this little hotel in a city called Egg. We check in and of course they knew we were coming but for some reason or another they didn't turn on the heat in Howard and Tom's room while my room was like the honeymoon suite. It was warm and toasty and they were freezing their butts off."

Tom and Lander went out with the group from Intamin manufacturing and Glosser stayed behind to get some sleep. After spending the better part of the night on the town, they came back to the hotel, woke up Glosser and proceeded "to eat and drink everything in my mini-bar and hung around until they were sure I was totally awake."

By that time Glosser was rested and ready to party, but Tom and Lander said good night and went back to their room to go to bed. A snowstorm hit later that night and it was still snowing the next morning as the three made their way to the Zurich airport. Their flight to Milan, Italy where they had appointments to visit several Italian manufacturers was delayed for an indefinite period.

I Want to Go Home

TP wanted to take the next flight home because he didn't want to get stuck in Europe and miss the Super Bowl. Howard was insistent on going to visit Zamperla, a major advertiser at the time and kept reminding Tom that was why they were there. While those two were debating, Glosser disappeared and came back with arrangements for them to travel by train instead. "We had very little time and we rushed to the train station. We were schlepping all this luggage and TP was moving rather slowly, because he was still recovering from his heart attack."

As they climbed on board the train, TP was sent ahead to find a cabin where they could all sit, while Lander and Glosser carried all the bags "through what seemed like 15 cars. We were sweating like pigs," Glosser recalls. When settled, they relaxed a bit and Glosser reached in his bag, pulled out two apples, gave one to Tom and started eating the other. "Howard looked at me and got really pissed because he did all the carrying and the work and Tom got the second apple."

Alfeo Moser, then of Soriani & Moser and now owner of Moser Rides, picked them up at the train station. Tom and Lander wanted to do some shopping in downtown Milan before they got down to business. That little side trip made them late to the Soriani & Moser factory in nearby Melara. A driver from Zamperla was scheduled to pick them up there after their interview and drive them to the Zamperla factory in Vicentina.

"We were running very late. Tom didn't feel like going to Zamperla that late, so he and I and the group from Soriani & Moser went out to dinner, while Howard went on with the driver," Glosser said. Howard got to Zamperla around 10 p.m., had a meeting, took a tour and was driven back to join the others, who were waiting for him because they had a driver ready to get them back to Milan for their flight back to the U.S.

FOOT IN MOUTH

"I first met TP in Germany. I was walking down the street with my wife Pat and the rest of the Americans on our tour. Tom turned around, saw Pat, and made a remark to Bill Alter, like, man look at her. We all laughed and I said hey, that's my wife. So today, I still kid him that my wife is his little secret girlfriend."

- Roy Gillian, Wonderland Pier

They all piled into the driver's Peugeot with Glosser and Tom in the back seat with some of the luggage. Thanks to the shopping trip in Milan, the back seat and the trunk of the little car was packed. Lander sat in the front seat next to Georgio, the driver. It's dark. It's snowing. It's cold.

About an hour into the trip, they got a flat tire. "It's so cold outside that nobody wanted to get out, but Georgio and Howard do and I'm pretending I'm asleep and Tom is out like a light. They had to unload all the luggage to get to the spare and then neither one of them could get the lug nuts off the old wheel," Glosser remembers, laughing. It's about 2 a.m. and the group is still a couple hours away from Milan with their flight set for an 8 a.m. departure.

"I finally got out, took the lug wrench, jumped up and down on it and loosened the nuts and got back in the car," Glosser said. The other two changed the tire, loaded everything back in and all arrived at the hotel in time to freshen up and get about an hour nap before heading to the airport.

Now The Funny Part Begins

But this is where the "really, really, really funny part starts," Glosser notes. In those days in Italy you were not allowed to bring in or take out substantial amounts of cash and they nearly always checked you at the airport.

"Now remember, we were originally supposed to fly from Zurich to Milan and when you do that there's a form you fill out on the plane and it's no problem as long as you declare the amount of money you are bringing into the country," Glosser said. Because they went by train they weren't required to fill out the forms and made no declarations.

They arrived at the airport and were walking toward their gate, and Glosser is wondering whether they'll be stopped and checked for money of which he had a substantial amount. "Howard is ahead of us with a shopping bag full of the Gucci stuff he bought for his wife and Tom and I are straggling behind. I see these two official looking guys walking toward us and I knew they were the guys that check for money. I reached into my left pocket, took my cash, which amounted to about $2,000 walked up behind Howard and dropped the cash into his shopping bag without anyone noticing it." He also tried to pass off the rest of the money in his right pocket but the officials saw the attempt and stopped them. Both ended up in the interrogation room and underwent a complete search of their person and their bags.

Enjoying a brew in Germany are Dan Glosser, TP, German concessionaire Roland Koch, and Bill Alter.

No Fun Being Detained

Glosser whispered to Tom that they might end up being detained and might even have to go to jail meaning that TP would miss the Super Bowl. Sweat starting pouring off Tom and according to Glosser, he "was very nervous, somewhat scared and absolutely beside himself."

By then it was apparent that they had too much cash. However, it was Glosser's quick thinking that saved the Super Bowl for TP. "I said look, we were out drinking last night and my friend Tom here, and the other guy that was with us, drank too much and they gave me their cash for safe keeping. That's why I've got it all on my body because it's for three guys and not just mine."

The officials finally accepted that explanation and the two walked out onto the concourse and found Lander who had been looking for them. "I put my hand in the shopping bag and I take my money back. He didn't even know it was in there," Glosser laughs.

> **TP on TP**
>
> *"Being in sales is one job I would never want. I don't think I could ever enjoy doing that. I need to travel more than an AB salesman does."*
>   *- Tom Powell*

Lost in a Doniker

TP went back to Germany in September 1984 to attend the Oktoberfest in Munich, a trip that he took 10 times during his AB years.

Dan Glosser was once again valuable to TP because he knew all the German showmen and took Tom around and introduced him to them. It was perfect for Tom. He met new people, got a lot of stories, all while enjoying liter after liter of great German beer. That year, TP and Glosser were joined on their rounds at Oktoberfest by ride brokers Mel Eddy and Jim Glover. They started at 10 a.m. each day and drank their way through the beer halls and showmen's trailers.

By late afternoon on one particular day, the group had consumed several liters of high octane German beer and had enjoyed many shots of schnapps. They were feeling pretty good by the time the sun went down and they started walking down the midway to get a taxi to take them to the hotel. Tom sees the sign for the doniker (bathroom) and says he has to go.

"He handed me his camera bag and off he goes," Glosser recalls. "Well, 20 or 30 minutes goes by and there's no Tom. He doesn't come out. So I said, Mel, would you mind going and take a look to see where he is?" A few minutes later he comes back and reports that he can't find Tom.

Glosser then got worried because he thought Tom didn't know the name of the hotel. After searching for another 30 minutes, they gave up and headed to the hotel, hoping that Tom had found his way. Sure enough, he was there and it was his excellent memory that saved the day. "I remembered that Dan had said the hotel's name translated into something like the king's hound and I told the taxi driver that and he got me back," TP said.

How did they lose each other? On the fairgrounds, there are two types of bathrooms, one for defecation, one for urination. Tom was in one, they looked for him in the other and when Tom came out, Glosser and Eddy were no where to be found.

On another trip to Germany with several other showmen and industry leaders, the late carnival owner Hub Luehrs, his son Bill and TP decided to go out for a drink late one evening after most of the pubs had filled up.

> **DRINKING WITH THE BEST**
>
> "TP made quite a hit with the Germans he met on the grounds of the Oktoberfest in Munich. He could drink with them and they liked that. You know they like to sit, eat, talk and drink liters of beer and they just keep on going and going. Tom was in his element. He's always been good at that."
>
> — Dan Glosser

They found what looked like a crowded dive and the doorman attempted to turn them away, saying the place was full. Bill (Luehrs) promptly informed him that TP was the governor of the great commonwealth of Pennsylvania, and it would behoove him to make room. Hub got upset because Bill identified him as TP's chauffeur, but they got in.

Don't Follow TP

Karen Oertley, AB's Publisher and Editor-in-Chief, remembers that Tom's ability not to find his way around was legendary by the time she started traveling with him in the early 1990s. "I remember flying to Europe with him and knowing in advance that I could not think for a minute of counting on him because he has absolutely no sense of direction," she recalls.

On one of their first joint trips, Karen forgot her own advice of never trusting TP's directional abilities. "We were slogging through an airport and I was just kind of following along behind him and we walked and walked and walked and had probably been going about 15 to 20 minutes and he turned around and he said, do you know where we're going? And I said I'm following you. He's like I don't know where we're going."

Oertley laughs that the "tough" TP never sleeps on the plane on long trips to Europe. "We would fly to Germany, which is a good eight, nine hour flight and Tom would sit straight up in his chair the entire time with a Scotch in his hand and he would read newspapers. He never dozed off and never really seemed to watch the movie. He would sit there and read every little box score and every tiny little piece of sports information. He kept his glass full the whole time and really never seemed the worse for the wear at all."

Tom was careful not to drink the water when he visited Mexico City in September 1991 to visit that city's new Sports Palace and the National Auditorium. However, he still got sick and couldn't figure out why. Finally someone suggested that it was the ice that he always mixes with his Scotch. "I know it wasn't the Scotch because that has never made me ill before," TP responded.

While there, he was invited to a gala performance of Cantata Escenica and Carmina Burana at the rededicated National Auditorium, operated by Ogden Services. To Tom's chagrin, the performance turned out to be a ballet. "I don't think I ever sat through a ballet before, and I know I never will again. Luckily, it lasted only one hour."

Rod Stewart, the imposter, croons a few for the gullible TP and John Hobbs.

Have I Told You Lately?

In fall 1996, TP and Christine, Johnny Hobbs and his wife Libby and several other couples traveled to Dublin, Ireland to attend the Notre Dame vs. Navy football game and ended up attending a reception at Ambassador Ann Kennedy Smith's house held for the two teams and their entourages.

Notre Dame beat Navy 54-27, which of course made TP's group happy, but the real excitement began when it was time for pub-crawling. Following the game, they went to Jury's Bar in Dublin and there sat who they thought was rock singer Rod Stewart.

Having no qualms about talking with anyone, TP introduced himself and they started talking about Nashville where "Stewart" had been the previous week. After a few pints and even more stories, the two said goodbye to each other, only to meet in another pub a couple days later. When TP and his group walked in, the Stewart imposter motioned them over. He drank and sang with the group, told TP that Elvis was his all-time favorite entertainer and that his all-time favorite country song is Bobby Bare's "500 Miles From Home." Before they said their good byes, the men had Stewart croon to their wives, his hit, "Have I Told You Lately That I Love You?"

It was a couple weeks later when AB reporter Ray Wadell was looking at the photos of TP and "Stewart" when he noticed that the Rod Stewart TP had met and drank with and sang with didn't have a mole on his face, as does the real Rod Stewart. TP had devoted a good portion of two columns before he realized he had been played for the iggy by the imposter. He never informed his readers of the musical scam.

27

TP'S ANNUAL VISIT TO SCRANTON

Each year in honor of his July birthday, TP visits his first true love, Scranton, Pa., his hometown. More specifically, he and Christine visit Bellevue, the small Irish community where he was born and raised.

He has proven to be a loyal son of Bellevue say his friends. Neil Regan, a Scranton funeral director, has been a friend of TP's since childhood and is delighted to see him each year.

"Tom is one of those unique individuals who works very hard at keeping friendships alive," Regan said. "Here's a guy who has been just about everywhere in the world but he feels most comfortable back here in his old neighborhood shooting the breeze with people that he grew up with 50, 60, 70 years ago."

Regan said while many people are not able to keep lifelong friendships alive, Tom has made it a point to keep his going. "We move along in our lives and we all get caught up in our families and in our own personal life. Sometimes we forget about things that were very important to us when we were young and some of those things are people, people that we encountered, people that we went to school with, people that we shared many moments with. Tom is not one who has forgotten his roots."

On To Bellevue

Tom has no family left in the Scranton area, but he still looks forward to visiting home. He's as loyal to that city as he is to his friends. He loves Arcaro's Pizza, and he loves to hang and drink with his long-time buddies. Hacky Fanning's Bar, once TP's favorite drinking spot in the world, was sold upon Hacky's death in 2000 and has since been renamed Shaughnessy's. While they'll still have a few drinks there, Christine and Tom don't call it home base as they did for years.

"We just went to Hacky's Bar and spent most of our time there, but when Hacky passed away, we started going to several other bars. There's a Ukrainian club down the street and we go there and just bum around. They

TP and childhood buddy, Charlie Manley in Scranton.

tell stories, old stories, the same stories over and over," said Christine.

TP and Charley Manley have known each other since they were both just out of diapers. They lived in the same neighborhood, went to the same schools, and remain friends to this day. Manley gets a call from TP when he's headed that way. "I then call all our friends and the place is packed when he shows up and we sit and drink and reminisce for days," Manley noted.

By the time the Powells get to Scranton, the crowd knows they are coming and out of tradition, they still start at Hacky's. "We always stay there long enough so people know we have arrived. People know my car and they watch for Tennessee tags. They already know we're coming, so they watch and when we arrive, they'll start hanging around and coming in even though they don't usually go there anymore."

The crowd has grown to love Christine as much as they do TP. One year he jokingly threatened to not bring her the following year. Everyone made a point to let him know he wouldn't be welcomed unless she was with him.

In 1984, TP thought it would be fun to visit the *Springfield Herald*, where he began his journalistic career at 75-cents an hour in 1951. After talking with several of his old buddies, the editors thought TP would make a good story. The shoe was on the other foot as he was interviewed for more than an hour. Afterward, TP laughed, "Have you ever tried to explain *Amusement Business* and what we do to someone?"

When it ran, the story gave TP a sense of accomplishment. "You know, you can travel the world over, but there's nothing that can beat recognition in your home town," he said. The adulation he receives from his life-long friends also serves as a validation for Tom, kind of like his parental community giving him a big, loving embrace.

A Community Hug

The locals are proud of TP, Manley said. "Here's this kid from the working class area of Bellevue who worked hard, put himself through college and now travels the world. You bet we are all proud of him. We were all equals here at one time, we know what it took for him to get where he is today."

TP and Manley and their third good buddy, the late Tom MacDonald spent most of their early years together. They played sports, went to dances, and hung out in the neighborhood. "We didn't smoke or drink or get in any trouble. In fact, we were all kind of dorks. I don't think Tom had his first beer until he was in the Army and he never did start smoking."

> **WE LOVE BELLEVUE**
>
> "We're Rough, We're Tough, We're from Bellevue. That's Enough!"
> - Charlie Manley, reciting neighborhood cheer

Tom's storytelling ability may have its roots in Bellevue as well. He would visit the Regan house where he would sit with Neil and his brothers Frank, Jack, Donald and Bob and listen to Frank Regan Sr. tell stories. "My father was a great storyteller and he would tell us all sorts of stories from the early years, from the turn of the century," Regan recalls.

Some of the stories were funny, some were true, and some were downright silly, according to Regan. One that he can recall that he said Tom particularly liked at the time went like this. "Poor Pat was puffing it out in the bedroom almost asleep and breathing his last breath when his wife Bridget brought him a bowl of chicken soup from the kitchen. As Pat was sipping away his eyes brightened and he said, Bridget, is that ham I smell cooking? Bridget said that it is, Pat. Finish your soup. The ham is for your wake."

Taking a Friend Home

In 1996, Don Sandefur joined TP and Christine for the July jaunt to Scranton. "We had the IAAM convention that year in Philadelphia, so I joined him in Scranton for a few days before the meetings were to begin," Sandefur said. "Those few days with him in Bellevue were the greatest times I have ever had with him, by far. I mean it is unbelievable and I got to see the real Tom Powell."

Sandefur was blown away by the neighborhood and by Hacky's bar. "It is a unique place. Literally everybody knows everyone's name in there. We'd go in, sit down, order a drink and that's all we did all day. I wanted to go out and see Scranton; no we're going to Hacky's. I finally convinced him to take a drive through the neighborhood. I wanted to see his high school. "So we drive out by his old high school and he says all right let's go back to Hacky's."

Sandefur loved the blue-collar rituals that he observed while being held captive by TP and the group in the bar. "Everyday at the same time, Hacky would pull up an empty stool to the bar, put a beer there, a shot, an ashtray, and some change. I'm looking around thinking to myself what in the hell is going on. Within 30 seconds some guy comes in, sits at the bar, hands Hacky a $5 bill, takes the shot, drinks the beer, has a cigarette, puts the cigarette out in the ashtray, takes the change in his pocket and leaves. And not a word was exchanged between the two."

Sandefur said it was obvious to him why TP goes home every year. "Everybody in there loves Tom and they consider him somewhat of a hero around there because he knows famous people and therefore Tom is famous. He's kind of revered in that neighborhood and you know, he definitely reveres that neighborhood."

Frank Arcaro, owner of Arcaro's Bar & Grill in Scranton makes TP's favorite pizza.

28

KISSES & HUGS IN HERSHEY

TP and Christine usually make a stop at Hersheypark each year on their pilgrimage back to Scranton. They stay at Hotel Hershey and are wined and dined for a couple of days by top officials of the park.

J. Bruce McKinney, who retired as President/CEO from Hershey Entertainment, said the dinners and the special fanfare when TP visits evolved out of his frequent trips to the park in the 1980s to do stories.

"We just kind of hit it off as both in friend-to-friend and business-to-business relationships and we wanted to do more for him than just host his visits to the park. We wanted to introduce him to the school, introduce him to the community, and more importantly introduce him to other people within the company. So we would have these VIP gathering for him," McKinney said.

It became an annual event. When Tom and Christine would visit Hershey officials would roll out the red carpet, have him stay at the hotel and arrange at least one major function or dinner. "We just did this as a kind of tribute to him and at the same time it was a case of a good family friend coming to town."

Franklin Shearer, now retired GM of the park, said that while TP enjoyed the attention, the food and the drink, he also enjoyed visiting with other staff members and taking a tour of the arena and the park. "I'd pick up Tom early in the morning at the hotel and take him on a grand tour of Hersheypark on a golf cart, showing him what was new for the season. He showed genuine interest in everything we were doing and would take methodical notes and have me stop frequently to take pictures," Shearer said.

A Special Training Course

Former Hersheypark GM Paul Serff, now CEO of the Texas Travel Industry Association, used to be part of those TP dinners and said everyone looked forward to TP's arrival knowing they would learn a great deal about the industry and about other parks while he was there.

In response to that, Serff printed up "Tom Powell, School of Intensive

Training" name tags for everyone. "I can't remember exactly how it started, but we truly felt that we were all members of the Tom Powell School of Intensive Training. Today, when TP shows up at Hershey, the executives still pull out the badges and wear them to honor him. "Tom was the master and we were all the trainees," Serff said.

Serff was in charge of what he called the Tom Powell Celebration Committee. In 1990, Serff took a big step and tried to get the U.S. Government to authorize an official TP Holiday. He sent a copy to TP as a birthday greeting. Serff wrote: "Dear Madam or Sir. Sorry I don't have your direct address, but I'm sure you're somewhere in Washington, D.C. At any rate, I hope this finds you in a receptive mood. My friends and I would like you to consider July 18 as a National Holiday. It is, after all, Tom Powell's birthday. What, you don't know who Tom Powell is?

"Just ask anybody who has ever been in discussions involving theme parks, fairs, carnivals, arenas, stadiums, race tracks, concessions, libations, sports of all kinds, or any subject remotely connected with any of the above, and I'm sure they know the name Tom Powell." Serff goes on to explain how well traveled TP is and pointed out there are few bars he hasn't visited.

"He rarely forgets a name or face and never forgets a good story. He's an accomplished photographer and I honestly believe he can write equally well with both hands. But most of all he has been a really GOOD FRIEND to the entertainment industry for a lot of years. We think that he deserves some special recognition. July 18th does not seem to be a very popular day for holidays. It falls somewhere between Fete Nationale in Belgium and Fete Nationale in France, but other than that, it appears to be an open unclaimed day.

"Well, thanks for listening. Please consider our request, and by the way, if you see Tom Powell, tell him his friends from Hershey said Happy Birthday." The letter was signed, "The Committee."

The Hershey contingent greeting TP on his birthday. From left are Lucille and Franklin Shearer, Sally and Bruce McKinney, TP, and Kathy and Paul Serff.

29

TP VISITS KNOEBELS

While in that part of Pennsylvania, TP uses the opportunity to visit his friends at Knoebels Amusement Resort and to partake in the National Ticket Company annual picnic that is held that time each summer.

> **WELCOME TO OUR PARK**
>
> *TP is a man who knows how to have fun and we love to have him visit with us at the park. He's quite the legend and we're proud to know him.*
>
> *-Dick Knoebel*

"The first time I met him he had been to the National Ticket Company clam bake, which used to be held at the Valley Gun and Country Club here in Elysburg," said Dick Knoebel, who owns the traditional amusement park with his family. In the late 1990s, the clambake was moved to the amusement park and of course, TP followed. Dick and TP, along with their wives, Barbara and Christine, have turned out to be good friends and often party together at the various conventions.

When it was time for Knoebel to put together a 75th Anniversary Celebration for his park in 2001, he insisted that TP be a part of it.

"We had this ceremony and I had my invited guests, visiting dignitaries, mostly politicians, say a few words from the stage and it was the typical stuff. Then Tom got up and really lightened up things. He was very good. He made some comments about me being with him in different parts of the world on some of the IAAPA tours, and then he read an original poem that he wrote about Knoebels. He took the word Knoebel, took the initials, and made a stanza out of each letter."

For years, the Knoebels, TP and Christine, Bob and Maxine Payne, and Bill Alter and his wife Jane Ann would meet for dinner and drinks at Cox's Restaurant in Elysburg the night before the National Ticket Company's clambake. Knoebel kept telling TP about a unique unlicensed bar out in the boonies that the locals call Caboodle Hollow. The establishment was operated by a 90-year old man and Knoebel told TP it never closed. It was the area's worst kept secret and everyone, including the police knew about it.

Knoebel recalls: "I wanted to get him out there to see the place and because the beers were like 15 cents each, but I couldn't get him out of Cox's. We finally got him in the car one night and drove up to this place. It's a long drive, very dark and mostly a dirt road. Oh God, it was dusty and when we finally got there it was so late they had closed. He has never let me forget it and he made me take him back to Cox's so he could continue drinking."

TP with Dick and Barbara Knoebel. Seated are Duke Smith and Carolyn Patterson.

30

LIVING AS A LEGEND

"I'm sure Tom doesn't consider himself to be a hero, because all he has done is devote his life to being his best and making the most of his talents. He has worked hard, enjoyed his vocation, been honest in his dealing with his fellow man, made friends, and become a friend to more people than most have had the opportunity to meet."

Those are the words of Don Patterson, of Virco, an industry provider of seating.

Even if people had never met TP in person, they felt they already knew him through his column. He was open, honest and let everyone know what Tom Powell was all about. If you read his column, you knew TP.

> **TP ON TP**
>
> *"A lady once called and asked me to write up a Final Curtain (what AB calls obituaries) for her so she could declare herself dead and not have to pay the IRS."*
>
> *- Tom Powell*

Being Tom Powell, the legend isn't always easy. People ask a lot of him, they try to get a lot from him and many hang on hoping that TP will somehow be of help to them. But it can also be fun being a legend. Free drinks, free food, free trips, free access and the opportunity to meet new people from all strata of society.

The most common favor people want from Tom are free tickets. "People call wanting tickets for events all over the country, and that is a pain most of the time. They know I know somebody and they expect a lot from me." In most cases, he'll take time to make a phone call to see what he can do, but through the years, he has become more particular for whom he will get tickets.

> **MARRIED TO A LEGEND**
>
> *"I don't think of him as a legend. I just think of him as Tom. He's simple but he can be very complicated but mostly he's just Thomas. There are no airs to him. There's no jealousy. He just kind of lives his own life and tries to do the best he can."*
>
> *- Christine Powell*

How Should a Legend Act?

So, what's a legend to do? While TP has the needed ego of a successful journalist and public figure, he does have a humble streak when it comes to this legend thing. "Don't forget I grew up in Scranton where they still call me by the hated nickname of Moldy. I am surprised and totally and sincerely flattered that some people call me a legend. I have never had a big head and don't think I ever will."

He never liked the named Moldy and hid it from his friends and family once he settled in Nashville. Actually, the name doesn't mean anything, he claims. Everyone else had a nickname, so his buddies gave him that one.

In 1971, a year before he joined AB, TP made his first trek to a World Series game, as a sports reporter for Nashville's daily newspaper, *The Tennessean*. He was "thrilled to the gills" to be working while attending something he had loved since childhood, baseball. Needless to say, he was humbled. "I couldn't help thinking how my dad would flip if he knew his son was sitting up there with press from across the world."

TP Superstar

TP is nothing short of being a superstar to the people in the carnival industry. "You know, everyone refers to Tom as a legend and I think he really is. Sometimes that word is used too loosely, but he really is," said concessionaire Bobby Leonard who has known TP since the mid-1970s. Leonard said TP stands out from all the others because he's "jam up and jelly tight, and that's good. He's an asset to our industry. We're lucky to have him."

David Conedara, another concessionaire agrees. "He's an ambassador for our business. He's got personality and he gets along with everybody. I've never heard anybody say a bad word about him, never. He's always fun to be around."

On being legendary, good friend and carnival owner Bud Gilmore says of his buddy, "He's a great legend for not only the amusement business industry but for the *Amusement Business* newspaper as well.. Not only does everyone know him, he knows everybody. That's so important in today's business world. Our industry is a people business and if you don't know the people, you don't do the business."

"TP wasn't quite a legend when I first met him in the '70s, but it didn't take too long for him to become one," said concessionaire Alieta Klinger.

She speaks for the carnival industry when she says that TP is "not just an editor of a newspaper that writes about us. He is part of us and he understands it all and he understands us."

> **MORE THAN A LEGEND**
>
> "I think legends build themselves and I think he did. You know, it's not only the position he has with AB. He is a good person. It isn't the position that made him who he is."
>
> - Concessionaire Alieta Klinger

31

TP THE TOASTMASTER

TP was the first to introduce both Randy Travis and Garth Brooks from a stage in Nashville. Both incidences occurred during the annual AB-sponsored showcase for talent buyers who were in town for either the Country Music Association's CMA Week or the events that led up to the annual Fan Fair, now known as the CMA Music Festival.

It was at these events that TP also perfected his public speaking skills. AB Publisher Walt Heeney came up to Tom one afternoon in 1974 and told him that he would have to be the MC for the AB Showcase that night because the regular guy wasn't going to be able to make it.

TP recalls: "I said, well, I've never done that but I'd be glad to do it. I remember Bob Luman was on and we had Harry Blackstone Jr. the magician and there were several other acts I can't remember. Luman did his thing and Harry Blackstone did his and I was ready to announce the next act when they whispered from off stage that I had to kill some time. That time turned out to be 30 minutes."

He told the crowd what was going on and then proceeded to tell every joke he could remember. Then he got an idea and to this day, he thinks its one of the funniest things he has ever done in front of a crowd. "I said you know it just dawned on me. Most of you people don't even know who I am. My name is Ray Pilszak and I'm the sales director of *Amusement Business* and you've got to meet our new editor. Tom Powell is the nicest guy you're ever going to meet. I'm pouring it on what a great guy Tom Powell is and I was able to kill about 10 minutes with that. He's the most wonderful guy. Nobody knew me back then so it worked."

Garth Brooks Showcases

Buddy Lee Attractions was one of the first talent agencies to provide acts for the AB Showcase. "We presented a lot of acts through the years and Garth Brooks was one of them we were very happy to showcase. The first time anybody ever saw Garth Brooks was at the AB party," said Tony Conway, president of Buddy Lee Attractions.

But even though TP had the power of the stage with him, he had his share of hecklers from the first time he ever walked on stage at those showcase parties. "During all those years I was master of ceremonies, I was the only one on stage who ever got booed," TP laughs. "And most of it came from that peanut gallery in the balcony."

That peanut gallery was full of TP's friends including Frank Jirik, George Smith, Earl Duryea, Paul Buck, Mike Pierce, and Dick Geyer. "We would sit up there in a corner every year and we'd be his nemesis. We'd yell out to give him the hook," said Dick Geyer. "Give him the hook. Get him the hell off the stage. We'd aggravate the shit out of him."

But in true TP fashion, he wouldn't simply get on with the show during the heckling. "At first he didn't know who it was, but when he looked up and saw who was in his face he'd say, Geyer, shut the hell up and let me get my job done."

Uh, Uh, Huh?

In 1989, prior to going on stage to introduce the acts for the AB Showcase, TP talked with them to see how they wanted to be introduced. When he talked with the guys from Riders in the Sky, a group he knew and liked, he asked what they wanted him to say about them. "Simply as America's favorite band," they said.

When it was time for their introduction, TP got up to do so. "It was then, for the first time, at least that I can remember, in my checkered career that I drew a blank," TP recalls. "As I stood there, I could hear the band members behind the curtain, saying 'Yeah, without further ado, now what?'" The soundman helped out and TP finished up the introduction.

In November 1989, TP was asked to speak a few words at the funeral of his long time friend, Danny Fleenor of the Hurricane Hell Drivers and later a fair manager. He recalled the time Fleenor tried to get him to ride with him during a show, an offer TP immediately declined. He also brought about many smiles when he said. "During all the years that Dan was driving, he was following a straight path to heaven."

Geyer invited TP to address his colleagues during an International Association of Assembly Managers district meeting in Rapid City, S.D., where Geyer was manager of the Rushmore Plaza. The event in which he was to talk took place up the hill toward the big faces on Mount Rushmore. After the long walk and as TP approached the podium, his quick wit kicked in. "Look," he exclaimed pointing to the carvings. "I've always heard this was breathtaking, but my breath was gone before I even saw it."

Many, Many Engagements

During his career at AB, Tom has been the master of ceremonies, the after dinner speaker and convention keynote speaker at hundreds of industry functions.

In 1993, he was invited to be master of ceremonies at the annual banquet and ball of the combined meetings in Las Vegas of the International Association of Fairs & Expositions, the Outdoor Amusement Business Association and the Showmen's League of America, whose first president was Buffalo Bill Cody. He was humbled by the request and told organizers that "only in America could the son of a coal miner be toastmaster of such a prestigious event."

His speaking ability has put TP in several unique positions. "When I retired in 2000 and I was putting together my program I only wanted three speakers. One was a classmate of mine at the Milton Hershey School here in town, one was a good friend of mine from Hershey Foods, and one was Tom Powell," Bruce McKinney said about his retirement from Hersheypark. "Tom was the only industry person I asked to be a speaker recognizing that there are tons of people that I knew through the years but he was the one that I wanted to be there and he did a very appropriate job," said McKinney.

He wrote out the speech for me and had it framed and I have it on my wall. I only take it down once a year when I replace it with the hockey schedule for the Hershey Bears. When hockey season is over, the speech goes back up."

TP and Danny Davis, a good friend and the leader of the Nashville Brass.

32

FIRST & ALWAYS A JOURNALIST

TP is a celebrity journalist. He's recognized wherever he goes within AB's coverage areas and he loves it. Who wouldn't?

He's Mr. AB to most of the long-time readers of the magazine. While never being the owner or the publisher, TP has always been better known than whoever ran the magazine. Many people have mistakenly introduced Tom as the owner or the publisher of the magazine.

His notoriety as an industry insider sometimes overshadows his journalistic ability, but he is a dedicated journalist first. "It's a unique situation to be in because I'm so identified with the industries we cover, but I'm definitely a journalist first. We not only cover the industries, but we are an integral part of them. That carries even a larger responsibility than being just a journalist covering a story," TP said.

If he lost his full time job for some reason, TP says he would probably spend time at trade shows and would write freelance stories. He wouldn't accept any of the hundreds of jobs he would probably be offered to join a carnival or a fair.

"Tom is in love with the paper. With most people it's like a job but to Tom that paper has been his life for so long and I think it shows. He truly loves all the people in the business. He truly cares about the paper," said TP's wife Christine. He claims he would never have come close to what he has now if he had just stayed with a daily newspaper. TP is a believer that one gets back what he puts in.

A Proud Member Of The Fourth Estate

Journalists have traditionally gotten a bad rap through the years as sensationalists and most recently in 2003 by the New York Times and the Jayson Blair scandals. But while the lack of ethics in those actions bothered TP, he never lost the pride of being able to call himself a journalist.

"I wear the title proudly and always have," he proclaims. "Just because there are a few bad apples in the bunch, just because one cop is bad, doesn't mean they all are."

Even the in-depth coverage about Ted Williams' body being frozen with his head in one tank and his body in another, didn't phase TP. "I'm sure, in some way that it deserves the press it got, but I always tune out. I want to think of him only as one of the greatest hitters of all time."

For a short time after getting a college degree in accounting, TP was an auditor with the General Accounting Office, working on the Department of Agriculture audit in Washington D.C. It was a job that makes his AB journey that much sweeter. "I had trouble staying awake every day. Like many of the other civil service employees, I was a clock watcher. I now love what I'm doing. In fact, most times I think it's the best job in the world."

Concessionaire Bill Lordy thinks TP has us all fooled. "He loves his job, he loves the industry and he loves being a journalist. We all actually think he's working when in fact, he's just having one great time."

Being An AB Journalist

Editorial coverage at AB during the 70s and 80s could best be described as grass roots. The reporters took their own photos, wrote their own stories, and in most cases, booked their own travel and hotel reservations. If a trip was required under 500 or so miles, chances are travel would be by car.

It was an environment in which TP thrived. "It was much more down to earth and kept us a lot closer to the industry and to each other," Ray Pilszak, former AB sales manager recalls. "We would travel a lot together and carpool to different events. Once we got there, he would go one way and I would usually go another."

Petty differences certainly occurred during the days when AB staff traveled together in the same car, and then after a long journey, they would have to room together in the same hotel room. Pilszak said those differences caused bickering, but in the long run, they brought the staff closer together, kind of like brothers and sisters.

Tom was the pickiest of the group, Pilszak claims, so to keep peace, most of the time things were done the way TP wanted them done. "We pretty much went to eat wherever Tom wanted to go. I wasn't as fussy about the food. Tom usually likes the basic meat plate with three vegetables. I tried countless times to get him to try something new and he always said no."

SMILE!!!

"I don't know if I want to call it photojournalism because we weren't great photographers but we did agree that a lot of times a photo could tell the story and TP loves to take pictures."

— Howard Lander

Say Cheese, Please

The adage that a picture says a thousand words was proven years ago at AB. Prior to TP's arrival, photos were never an important part of industry coverage. TP soon found that everybody loved having their photos in the paper and people pictures soon became a stalwart of coverage.

However, the actual taking of a successful photograph was sometimes just out of the reach of TP. There are dozens of stories out there about Tom having problems taking photos. While he loved taking pictures and probably took more than any other reporter at the newspaper, his photo skills were definitely below all his other noted abilities.

Dick Knoebel of Knoebels Amusement Resort in Elysburg, Pa., remembers the time TP showed up "just as we finished putting in a new funnel cake stand. He wanted to take a picture of it along with the staff. He had the flash on the camera backward and every time he'd take a picture it would just flash in his face," Knoebel laughed. Despite that more than common SNAFU (especially for TP) a few photos turned out and were published.

Another time, while waiting for his baggage on the way to the amusement park trade show in Dallas, TP spotted country music entertainer Jimmy Dean. The star agreed to have his picture taken with a few park executives who were also in the baggage claim area. TP shot several, as he always did, and thanked everyone. As he walked away, he had "this terrible feeling that I didn't have any film in the camera. I couldn't rest until I checked to see if I had film in there, so I decided to unload it, even if I only had those two shots on an entire roll. Sure enough, my worst suspicions were confirmed."

That no-film scenario happened enough times that when other AB photogs were taking pictures, people would ask if, unlike TP, they had film in their camera.

Weak batteries were also the culprit for a blown photo shoot on several occasions. When his flash would fail to go off, he would assure the people around him there was no problem. "That's OK, we have a guy in the darkroom that can fix anything," he said. And in most cases, he was right.

A True Balancing Act

TP made it an art to hold a drink in one hand while focusing and triggering the camera with another. It was an art not overlooked by those he was photographing. Attending Oktoberfest in Munich in

Being TP is a true balancing act.

1984, TP gave a short lecture to several park and carnival owners on how you could take a drink, snap a picture, write down the identification, take another drink, shoot another photo, etc.

One year during the Greater Tampa Showmen's Association Banquet, Pilszak lent his camera to the cause when TP needed to take a picture late in the evening and didn't have his with him, a rare occurrence in itself. TP took Pilszak's camera, lined seven people up for a photo, and then couldn't get the camera to work. Pilszak and TP both labored over the camera to get it to work, but TP never did get the photo. Dead batteries were once again the culprit. On returning home, he got a letter from showmen Jean Clair who along with several others, witnessed the aborted photo attempt that night.

> **A FRIEND INDEED**
>
> *"To be TP's friend means you must be willing to work. He won't hesitate asking you to hold his drink while he takes a photo and then asking you to hold his camera while he writes down the names."*
> - Bill Lordy, Elephant Ear concessionaire

Caught In The Act Of Bumbling

"Dear TP. About a dozen of us show folks were entertained for a few brief, shining moments at the Tampa banquet, watching two middle-aged handsome guys trying to load a camera. They were great! They had the camera upside down and inside out, constantly grabbing it from each other, using stickpins and toothpicks, trying to release the winder. We imagined that the winder was stuck due to worn out batteries. I mean these two should have done a battery commercial. Thanks for the yuks, Tom Powell and aging sales director Ray Pilszak." It was signed, "Jean Clair and entertained friends."

Following a Neil Diamond concert in 1985 at the Seattle Center, TP was backstage hoping to get a photo. Diamond wasn't able to make time for the photo, but not to waste his time or the opportunity, he asked two of the promoters, John Meglen and Sal Bonafede of Concerts West, if he could get their photo. They laughed, and agreeing they were poor substitutes for Diamond, threw their arms around each other and smiled. "Nervously I kept hitting the button to snap the photo, and three times it failed to click. It had frozen on me again," TP said, adding that there really was a silver lining to that situation.

"It was bad enough I missed out on the photo of those two guys who had been so helpful, but I thought how much more frustrating it would have been if Diamond would have posed and the same thing occurred."

That prophecy came true in 1992. Backstage at a Diamond Concert at the Capital Center in Landover, Md., TP and Diamond struck a pose and Tom's wife Christine tried to snap the photo, but the battery had died.

Diamond broke the silence. "Better call Triple-A, your battery is dead," he quipped. The day was saved when Diamond's publicist took a photo and sent it to TP.

He Always Gets His Photo, One Way Or Another

When TP was once caught needing a photo but didn't have his camera, his intuition kicked in. A

> **THE IMAGE WAS RIGHT**
>
> *"TP always seemed larger than life. He struck me as a real newspaperman. I mean he was real, if anyone carried around an image of what a hard-driving newspaperman was all about, I think he fit that image."*
>
> *- Wayne McCary*

number of years ago, one of his favorite entertainers, singer Roger Whittaker performed a concert in Nashville at the Tennessee Performing Arts Center. He found himself backstage with Whittaker without a camera, but made plans to catch up with him in the morning at the airport to take the photo.

Bruce Lahti, Whittaker's manager had given TP the wrong flight time and he arrived two minutes before the gate was to be closed. He flashed his business card, he flashed his smile, and explained his mission. Thanks to his persuasive personality, the gate attendant walked him onto the plane and he got his photo of Whittaker sitting in First Class. With airport security restrictions being as there are now, TP would have missed that one in today's world.

The Dodger's Tommy Lasorda visits the Nashville Palace whenever he comes to Music City. One night, he showed up unexpectedly and not only was TP there, but Hobbs' grandchildren were as well. "I said, Tom, how about getting your camera and take a couple of pictures of my grandkids with Tommy," Hobbs said. Obligingly, Tom took out his camera and started taking pictures.

Hobbs laughs at what happened. "I'm looking at the flash and it's shooting backwards. It's hitting the wall behind Tom instead of on the group. I said, Tom, I don't know anything about cameras but I know one thing, that flash is on backwards." By the time that fact was brought to his attention, he had taken a roll of film and had none left. Hobbs never did get his family photos.

Life Has Been Good To Me

All journalistic jobs offer some kind of perks, but the niche position TP has created offers perks that few can only imagine. "I've had wonderful opportunities that my job has allowed me to experience. Opportunities I would probably have never had if I were not in this position. I have found myself sitting in suites at Super Bowls and Final 4s, treated like royalty at major events, meeting my sports heroes, going elbow to elbow with some of the biggest names in show business. I've met President Clinton. Yes, there have been some great perks," he said.

Virtually every successful journalist feels he or she has the "Great American Novel" inside waiting to get on paper. TP would like to write one about being born and being raised in Depression-era Scranton, Pa., and growing up to be the man he is. He would call the novel TP on TP. He sees the opening line in that novel being "I was born in 1933 to a coal miner." The last line would be "Thanks for everything. It has been a sensational, wonderful trip."

The Right Guy For This Job

Tom's journalistic notoriety and legendary column in AB have been quite beneficial for the entire industry. Howard Lander thinks the 1970s through the 1980s was the perfect time for AB to have a strong personality and a legend such as TP editing and fronting for it.

"Tom's column, which was legendary in its own right, was what we needed. It was part of that relationship. You know I remember it got to a point I had to keep telling him that a column is supposed to be a column. It's not supposed to jump two or three times. I mean Tom would get carried away and was really into it. I kept saying you can't do this and I would pick up the paper and there would be his column jumping two or three times. I finally said, Tom, I asked you not to do this and he said, yeah, but you never ordered me," Lander recalls.

Former carnival owner and now ride builder Bob Childress thinks TP is a valuable workhorse for AB. "He's always working. Always doing his job." Wherever he is he's making pictures or interviewing somebody. He's also having a good time, but he's always on the job. I've never seen a journalist work that hard before."

Roy Gillian, former mayor of Ocean City, N.J. and owner with his family of the famous Wonderland Pier in that city, says he appreciates a good journalist, after dealing with many unfair ones during his public life. "He has done many stories with me and he has always quoted me correctly," Gillian said. "That's a relief after being quoted wrong by other newspaper people most of my life."

TP's journalistic style can be deceiving to those who don't know him. He's casual, laughs a lot and doesn't always write down most of what a person says. Yet, he is seldom called for inaccuracy.

The Man Has His Own Style

Father John Vakulskas Jr., a carny priest from Dow City, Iowa, a public figure himself, sees TP's style as suitable to TP himself. "It's his own style and I've never seen any other reporter with it. He's caring but yet he's exact. When he reports on something he's very factual. As a person he's caring, cordial and fun, but as a professional he's very accurate and to the point."

Writing teachers tell students to write what they know most about and as result, they'll be better writers. Tom has proven that. First as a sports writer, now as an amusement industry reporter he has always written about what he knows and loves best. He's an expert on carnival owners. He knows how far to go with them and how to talk with them, and they all know to have a bottle of Scotch and two drinks ready when he walks in, and they all want him to come back.

He drinks with them all and in doing so, he gets his story and gets information they wouldn't tell anyone else. If you sit down with a man you like and you're having a drink or two with him before long he'll loosen up a little and say things he might not have said in a boardroom or from behind a desk.

Wayne McCary says Tom reminds him of Jimmy Breslin. "Both represent a breed of reporter that you're not going see the likes of again. What TP brought to the industry was not only the preponderance of articles and news stories but it was clear that people would let their hair down with Tom. Because of that he had a greater perspective about people in our industry than you might otherwise expect to get. People respect him but at the same time I think that he has had a unique perch to assess people in the business."

McCary says Tom has the edge because he knows those he writes about in the context of where they work, not from behind the computer but in the field, on the front line.

Carnival owner Jimmy Drew of the James H. Drew Exposition said TP is so successful and is considered such a good journalist is because he "becomes the industry when he interviews and writes. He puts himself in the situation and with his vast knowledge, he knows the questions to ask. If you haven't been there and done it and know the business, there is no way you can ask good questions. TP's beyond all that."

Both McCary and Drew feel TP has raised the level of the fair and carnival industries through his informed writing. "He has enlightened many about the good that our industries do," Drew said.

Lander said the publication was always known for its hard-drinking editors, but TP added a new dimension. "Tom fit that mode, but what he added to it was his ability to relate to all different levels of the business. He is a prolific writer. You know, it's hard to find an editor that took a camera and was eager to take pictures of everyone. That's the difference. He didn't think he was too good to do any of that."

TP Only, Please

Of course, Tom can't do all the writing the newspaper needs, but it's not unusual today for another AB reporter to call up someone for a story and be rejected, only to hear the words "No, Tom Powell will be the only one that will interview me."

In 1981 he attended a meeting in New York of all editors from the various publications that Billboard Publications Inc. owned. It was a management seminar and TP learned during those three days that he worked too much. It's a distinction between what they call management work and technical work, not technical in the sense it's complicated, but that it's the day to day routine stuff. "I should do something about that, but I'm a journalist. I can never see myself visiting somebody and not doing stories and taking pictures," said TP.

John Graff, now retired president and executive director of the International Association of Amusement Parks & Attractions, once questioned TP on whether Minnesota Fats was really still alive. The famed pool player was indeed alive, albeit more than 90 years old, living in Nashville and a frequent visitor to Tom's favorite bar, the Nashville Palace. TP took Fats' picture, put it in AB and mentioned he was doing that for Graff's benefit and to prove a point.

Graff responded: "Your dogged pursuit of the truth is an inspiration to young aspiring journalists and an example of tenacious investigative reporting at its finest. I stand corrected."

Don Sandefur and TP enjoy a cigar at The Nashville Palace.

33

LEARNING THE PERSONAL SIDE

As a seasoned journalist, Tom didn't have to worry about his writing or his journalistic skills when he reported for work at AB. The instincts were there and were never an issue as the life-long journalist began his new journey at AB.

When he attended the International Association of Assembly Managers (IAAM) convention in San Diego in July 1972, a month after he started with AB, it was only industry knowledge that TP lacked and it didn't take him long to get his arms around that.

It was at that convention that he began to realize what trade publishing was all about. "People came to me and thanked me for what AB had done for them over the years. I knew we covered the industry from a business standpoint, but it was there that I realized that an important part of that coverage were the people behind the stories." Ticketmaster's Donna Dowless thinks TP's emphasis on people helped distinguish *Amusement Business* as the friendly and professional trade publication. At their prime, "TP and AB was the perfect partnership. TP knew the industry and the people and the publication served as a vehicle for him to use that knowledge to not only chronicle the industry but to promote it as well."

Looking back over the thousands of stories he has written about all facets of the industry, TP recalls that his stories as well as all the stories that ran while he was in charge, were positive, people-oriented stories. "During

---

WINNING FRIENDS

"I was boycotting the publication and didn't want anything to do with it because of the previous management team. Then TP and I drank together and we talked and he said everybody was new and suggested that I meet Howard Lander. I did, I ended up liking them both, and as they say, time heals all wounds. I'm glad we ran into each other. TP was the catalyst for bringing me back into the fold."

— Dan Glosser, amusement ride broker

all the years I was editor I don't think we ever said anything negative about anybody. Anyone who ever got fired we gave their side of it and let them resign, so to speak, if that was what they wanted."

Forging Life-Long Friends

The 1972 IAAM Convention was the first for both TP and for Thaxter Trafton, then a building manager. They quickly became friends and have remained so for more than 30 years. It's a relationship built between two men with a lot in common. "We weren't together for more than five minutes when we first began talking about sports," Trafton pointed out. "We have a bond built on our passion for sports. It's what brought us together and what has kept us together."

TP is loyal to the fault, according to Trafton. "He's never gone south on a friend or on our industry. If you are a friend of Tom's it doesn't really make any difference what you do, he will be there supporting you. He has been a real pioneer in the way he has covered our industry."

Trafton isn't the first or only person to consider TP a pioneer, a moniker he doesn't think really fits him. "There were many real pioneers before me," TP said. "I just did my job to the best of my ability as I would have done no matter what profession I chose. That's the way I was brought up."

Don Sandefur, who met TP in 1973 at an IAAM convention, said he has been impressed through the years how TP always took the high road in dealing with people. By taking the high road Sandefur believes TP easily and quickly made a name for himself while helping establish AB as a major, trusted force within the industry.

Father John Vakulskas Jr., a priest serving the carnival community says that it is quite evident that TP loves his job. "It shows in his writings because this business is basically human beings serving human beings. We don't manufacture cars and we don't manufacture things. We manufacture fun and it's a people-to-people business. Tom portrays that aspect of our business in his writings."

According to Father John, a person "can see it in TP's eyes. Eyes are the mirrors of the soul and they show that he cares about people and that he cares about seeing the good in people."

34

HAIL FELLOW, WELL MET

"TP has a million friends and is a true hail fellow, well met," said Bob Reid, former building manager and Vee Corp. executive.

In the five dozen or more interviews conducted for this book, three consistent things surfaced. TP is truly an honorable person, TP is an asset to the industry and to *Amusement Business*, and TP's memory is one of his greatest gifts.

Auctioneer David Norton says TP's ability to remember names of people has a lot to do with his success and his popularity. "He can remember people, what towns they are from, the name of their spouses, what they do, and it just goes on and on," Norton said. "I'm in awe of that ability."

Carnival owner Bud Gilmore is still amazed with TP's ability to recall virtually everything. "The most important thing about him is his memory. I've sat and drank with him and things go on and on and he takes pictures and gets people's names, and the next morning I can't imagine how he could remember any of it but he never misses a thing."

Bud Gilmore an bar owner John Hobbs love to tell a particular story that illustrates TP's memory. Gilmore's carnival has played the Fryeburg (Maine) Fair for years and one summer, he invited TP to the fair to be a judge. Of course he got to meet the other judges but didn't have time to socialize with them or get to know them. One of the judges Tom was introduced to was Dwight Webber, who ran the little Blue Hill (Maine) Fair.

Playing Memory Games

When TP got back to Nashville, he did what he usually does after being out of town for awhile, he visits his friends at the Nashville Palace. Hobbs likes to show-off TP's wide knowledge of people by betting his bar patrons that TP will know somebody from their home town. Hobbs said he loses very seldom because "between all the people Tom knows and the fact that he hardly every forgets a name, it's a pretty safe bet."

Hobbs remembers one particular night with a smile. "There was a guy and his wife sitting at the bar and he started talking to me. I said where are you from? He said Blue Hill, Maine. I said do you have a fair in your town? He said yeah. I said do you know who runs it? He said yeah. I said I bet that guy with the beard sitting over there can tell you who runs it and who ran it before him," Hobbs recalls.

"The guy said that would be impossible and he bet me $5," Hobbs remembers. "So I called Tom over and the guy said he was from Blue Hill, Maine and asked TP who the fair manager was. "Tom smiled and in a fun way said 'Oh yeah, Dwight Webber." Hobbs recalls that the guy was a bit miffed and said "I'll be damned, what's the game, how many people do you take that way?" Hobbs told him to keep his $5 and go buy a couple more beers.

Learning Memory Skills

TP refined his memory while appreciating his life-long love of baseball. "I think Tom knows the batting average of every baseball player who ever played and he's got a remarkable memory. When you go to a ball game with Tom he can tell you who each player has played with, who he started with, what his batting average was each year. He loves baseball. I never knew a man that loves and knows baseball like Tom Powell does," said park industry veteran George Millay.

TIM ON TP
"Tom is not what you call mechanical savvy. In the early 1980s, he purchased a new Oldsmobile that burned diesel fuel. He had heard that burning diesel was cheaper than burning regular gasoline. In what he calls an expensive mistake, he pulled into a gas station and filled the tank with unleaded fuel, the first week he had it. It cost him so much to get it fixed that he figured it cancelled all the savings he had counted on for the life of the car."
- Tim O'Brien

"On the other hand, I am surprised that a man with that kind of memory gets lost so often. We were watching a baseball game one night at Greer Stadium in Nashville, and he got up to go to the bathroom and it took him nearly 30 minutes to find us again."

Hobbs said TP's memory helped him uncover a couple of phonies that came into the Palace one night. "These two boys came in and had World Series rings on from Cincinnati and I said did you play in the World Series? They said they did and go on talking for a little while. They were blowing a lot of steam to everybody.

"I got curious real quick so I asked their names. I said write them down so I'll be sure to get it right. I go and call Tom and I said look it up real quickly and tell me if these guys ever played. There's a book, the Baseball Encyclopedia that lists a player even if he only batted one time in the major leagues. Those guys weren't in it."

After talking with TP, Hobbs confronted the two. "I went over and I said you two guys are phony as hell and neither one of you have ever played in a game. I told them to quit telling all these people that crap. They said, 'well, we were bullpen catchers in the minor leagues.'" Tom, his memory and his reference book had spoiled the evening for those two guys. They quietly left the Palace shortly after their scam was exposed.

A Gentle Giant

Sometimes those who only know Tom through his column are often shy about approaching him. "Often I see people kind of standing off to the side wondering whether they should come up to me and talk. But once they do I'm sure they realize that I'm just a normal guy," TP said.

Dennis Carollo who with his dad, Albert, runs the Iron Mountain Iron Mine attraction in Michigan has been a friend of Tom's for years. Carollo notes that "In this industry he's in the spotlight because of the column and the newspaper. It's too bad some people think he's above them because believe me, he's really just one of them."

TP says he tries hard to treat everyone fairly, whether in conversation, in his column or in his news stories. "I have never done anything to intentionally hurt anybody while still not compromising the news," he points out.

Through the years, Father Mac has spent a great deal of time with TP and has seen the man in action, from industry trade shows to the carnival midway to bars in Germany. "People are attracted to him. They see him as a big shot and his reputation precedes him as being a person who can relate to anyone. TP will stop and talk to anyone and for those few minutes, Tom makes that person also feel like a big shot. He's good at that and it's not an act, he really enjoys meeting everyone," Father Mac says of his friend.

Bill Alter has logged many miles of travel with TP. "I have spent many days and evenings with Tom Powell and I can tell you that he is as comfortable with the most up tight and proper business person as he is with the roustabouts on the carnival midway." Midway food operator Little Richard Thomas says TP is a "real gentleman and never too busy to say hello to you. Boy, he remembers everybody. He's a good man."

A Man With People Skills

Another long time carnival friend, Bob Childress says he is amazed at TP's people skills. "He seems to know everybody's name and he's friends with everyone even if he doesn't know them. He just treats people nicely and people want to be with him and want to identify with him. He's just like a magnet."

Auctioneer Norton was standing in a crowd one day when someone looked over and saw a cluster of people surrounding TP and said "it looks like he has a little audience wherever he goes." Norton smiled. "The key word there was audience. The wrong word was little. He has a big audience wherever he goes and they all consider Tom a friend. People see TP as a celebrity and they live vicariously through him."

Sometimes TP is even surprised by his own notoriety. While checking into the William Penn Westin Hotel in Pittsburgh in 1993, the bellman looked at TP and said, "You look like Tom Powell of *Amusement Business*." Turns out Jerry Schaub, the bellman had been reading the newspaper for more than 50 years and is a balloon peddler at parades on weekends.

As the bellman took Tom and Christine to their room, he looked around, shook his head and called the front desk, explaining that the Powells were good friends of his and asked for an upgrade. Within minutes, they were in a new room.

Another example of how everyone seems to know TP, happened in spring 2003 when AB reporter Don Mooradian was waiting to serve on the Davidson County (Nashville) Grand Jury. At the end of the first week, the jurors filed into a courtroom presided over by Criminal Court Judge Randall Wyatt Jr. As Mooradian was sitting there, he thought he heard someone call out the name Tom Powell.

Mooradian looked around and not seeing TP, looked at the judge. "Do any of you know Tom Powell?" the judge asked again. He had seen Mooradian's place of employment on the form used to select jurors. "Yes, your honor. I work with Tom," said Mooradian. "Well, tell him I said hello," said the judge, who happened to be an old friend of TP's.

A Good Memory, A Big Plus

John Hobbs is a successful businessman, most recently opening up a family amusement park in Nashville. He knows what it takes to get the job done and he knows what impresses him about other businessmen. He says TP's people-skills are among the best he's ever seen. "The greatest thing about anybody is if they can remember everybody that walks up to them, and Tom's got that ability. He can remember better than any man I've ever seen in my life. If he meets you once he knows you the next time and knows how to spell your name," Hobbs said.

That skill goes a long way in business, Hobbs points out. "I've been with Tom all over the country and everywhere we go somebody will walk up that knows Tom Powell. To him, there are no big people and no little people; they are all the same."

Hobbs notes that in addition to his people skills, "Tom's got a damn good education. He's a very smart man. He's smart in common sense but has absolutely no mechanical skills. It's more in book sense and business sense. But as far as being able to get down and talk with anyone, there aren't any better."

35

ALWAYS THERE FOR HIS FRIENDS

The stories and the columns TP has written through the years have helped not only the industries that the newspaper covers, but a lot of individuals as well.

It's the efforts he has made behind the scenes, the times he has picked up the phone to make an introduction, the times he has been used as a personal reference that really distinguish TP as the friend.

Ray Pilszak, who has worked longer and closer to TP than anyone, says TP has a sensitive nature and wants to help those he likes. "He wants to help people in the industry. He's always open to listening to them."

In his own personal way, TP has nurtured not only the industry but those in it. Throughout his career he always gave people the benefit of the doubt and would always speak highly of them when interviewed by the national and international media. "I will always be true and loyal to my friends," said TP. "I would never betray a loyalty, to my death."

"If there was a way he could include something legitimately in his column or articles that would help someone, he would always be more than happy to do it. But during all the years, I never saw him show any unfair favoritism when it came to editorial coverage," Pilszak added.

Using His Network to Help Others

Being a legend means being well known and that has proven to be helpful for the newspaper, for TP, and for his friends. It has been a win-win for many for a long time. When Buddy Lee came to Nashville to set up a talent agency to book Hank Williams Jr., he had few, if any contacts with the fairs. He had never dealt with the media before. When confronted with a media question or a question on how best to use the media, he would call and TP would advise.

Tom also helped Lee get a foothold in the fair industry. At that time most country music acts played fairs and Tom introduced Lee as well as other agents who asked for help, to a myriad of fair managers and carnival operators, who were responsible for booking talent. Tom also helped Nashville's booking agents and promoters by writing stories on the artists or publishing stories on certain tours that the agency had on the road.

"Tom wrote that kind of stuff about everyone, but I think it especially helped us because we were new to the fair industry," said Tony Conway, current president of Buddy Lee Attractions.

Tom could have easily shown favoritism and could have easily made it point to help one person or company more than another. However, he was careful how he handled things and was fully aware of the influence his column and AB had at that time. "I never compromised AB's quality or integrity," he said. "I made it a point to treat everyone equally, big or small. There had to be a reason for a story and as everybody knows, everyone has a story to tell."

"Most of the fair people we dealt with then and that we still deal with get AB and they always talk about what they see or read. If they see a picture in there or if there's a story about one of our acts, they'll be the first one to mention it to us when we call them," Conway adds.

Tom was editor by the time Conway joined Buddy Lee Attractions in 1976. He soon became Uncle Tom to Conway. "I'd call him up and I'd say, Uncle Tom, I need to know who the guy is at this fair that I can call and sell some talent to. And right off the top of his head, he would know the guy I needed to talk with. Then he would often go one step further. He would say, 'I'm going to talk to him in a little while and if you want me to tell him you're a good kid and that you can be trusted, I will.' His endorsement was kind of a blessing. Once he told people they could honestly deal with me, they did, and many still do. You just don't have that kind of relationship anymore in this business," Conway said. "He's never been anything but a gentleman to me. Anytime I ever needed anything he was right there for me and he never asked for anything in return."

Due to the help he has handed out through the years, TP should definitely be considered as one of the best supporters and one of the best advocates the carnival, talent, and arena industries have ever had. He says he feels somewhat humbled when people tell him that, but he does agree with the assessment. "Yes, I do agree and I sure appreciate that people feel that way. My position enabled me to do that and I'm proud of it," he said.

A Walking Encyclopedia

"Tom's extensive knowledge of the industry is a treasured history that many of us have benefited from," said Donna Dowless, a former building manager, now with Ticketmaster in Florida. "He's the go-to guy when you have a question of who did this or who did that or who the contact is for a particular building or supplier. He is in tune with all aspects of the industry."

TP was "very instrumental in helping me learn more about the industry," Dowless said. "I called him up directly many times to ask specific questions, but I also learned from him by reading his column and by talking with him at the various conventions we both attended."

Dowless said TP's efforts at AB have helped people who didn't even know him, but were interested in learning about the industry. "By running so many photos, he put faces on people that the rest of the industry might not know if they didn't read the newspaper."

> **ON WITH THE SHOW**
>
> *"Good evening ladies and gentlemen, boys and girls. My name is Tom Powell, editor of Amusement Business. On behalf of Amusement Business and as a citizen of Nashville, I'd like to welcome the Greatest Show on Earth to Music City. Now sit back and relax and on with the show."*
> *- TP's script as Honorary Ringmaster when the Ringling Bros. and Barnum & Bailey Circus came to town*

Helping Park Executives

Being a proud Pennsylvanian, TP always liked Hersheypark. It was during his visits in the mid-to-late 1970s that park officials came up with a plan to expand the park. "When I first met him, we talked for hours. He talked about the industry in general and gave us a good idea of what was going on. He connected us with the park people we needed to know," said Bruce McKinney, now retired President/CEO from Hershey Entertainment Company.

Tom seemed eager to help the new executives. "He would say you have to meet this person and you have talk to this individual and when we were at functions he went out of his way to introduce us to people he thought we should know. Tom was clearly the link that helped us first realize how vast the park industry is and then the link to make sure we were a part of it."

Paul Serff, now CEO of the Texas Travel Industry Association, first met TP at an IAAPA convention while he was working at Hersheypark. "I was following Bob Payne around. Bob was our Director of Operations at Hershey and as far as I knew he knew everyone in the industry. One of the first people he introduced me to at that conference was Tom. With his booming voice and his incredible laugh and his positive attitude, Tom made the biggest impression on me of anyone that I met that year."

Dick Geyer, now President/CEO of the Wisconsin Center District, said TP introduced him to many, many people in both the fair and building management industries. "He would see me, introduce me to a group of people standing around and get us talking and feeling comfortable with each other and would then walk away. That's the kind of person he is."

Ray Pilszak said TP's recommendations were worth more than most people realized. "There were quite a few people who approached Tom to get a recommendation for a job, and a lot of people who were looking for a manager or director called him for a recommendation. People trusted his judgement."

Being known as a legend "isn't quite good enough to describe TP," said Thaxter Trafton, who has used Tom as a reference for every job he has landed since 1973. "I owe it all to him. I would never have gotten the jobs I have had if a man of TP's stature hadn't stepped forward for me. His name has power as a reference, that's for sure."

Fair Enough

Another benefactor of TP's loyalty and friendship is Wayne McCary., now CEO of the Eastern States Exposition in West Springfield, Mass. "Through the vehicle of *Amusement Business* people think they know Tom, but he has so much depth beyond that public persona and unless you really get to spend some time with him or come to know him personally, the special Tom Powell might escape you. He's a very loyal person."

McCary looks at TP as being a mentor to many and a great supporter of the professionals within all the industries in which he writes. "He clearly made a difference in my professional career, not through the media but as a person. He always took time for people and that was a lesson I learned from him," McCary noted.

> ### HAVE YOU TWO MET YET?
>
> *"Everyone in the industry eventually became Tom's friend. He is the only person I know of who could easily bring the industries together. As I got to know him, he wouldn't hesitate one second to introduce me to another park person or a carnival owner or an arena manager. He really brought us all together."*
>
> - Paul Serff

Parkie Meets the Carnies

John Graff, the retired president of the International Association of Amusement Parks & Attractions, said TP served as a "conscientious, effective bridge" between the carnival and the amusement park industries, even though he was more of a "carny" than a "parkie," he said. "He had a finger in each industry and is respected in each industry. He moved well between the two memberships and was able to write from a point of reason that certainly helped each understand the other."

In addition to helping people get jobs, he helped them understand other industries a bit better. George Smith was introduced to the late carnival owner Ray Cammack by TP. "I never thought carnies were too straight or on the up and up but this guy, Ray Cammack, would give you the shirt off his back. He was really one of the most genuine, honest, sincere people I ever met."

Smith, in what may be the understatement of the year, said that facility managers get fired regularly for all kinds of things out of their control. They could be doing a good job, but things like a power struggle at city hall, or a new mayor might take office and appoint his political cronies to replace a long-time facility manager. "There are so many bad raps we get ourselves into out here, that it was great to have TP there to tell the rest of the story to the rest of the industry. He saved the reputation of many of us."

TP visits his alma mater from which he graduated in 1951.

36

HOW SUITE IT IS!

Before making a name for himself on the carnival midway, TP made a mark in the arena, stadium and convention center industry. His first road trip for AB in 1972 was to the convention for the association that most of the industry belonged, the International Association of Assembly Managers (IAAM). (The association changed its name from "Auditoriums" to "Assembly" in the early 1990's.) It was there AB's and TP's reputation both grew quickly and strongly.

AB was the first publication and for the longest time, the only publication to chronicle the building and venue business. During TP's earliest days of covering the industry, he was thrown in with the rest of the "Press" and he felt that was a negative since many building managers weren't always on the best of terms with their local media. He knew that to be effective, AB would have to be thought of in a different light.

It took several years before he was accepted as something more than another member of the press, and in so doing he became an advocate as well as a chronicler of the industry. "TP was the first journalist who was allowed to attend our meetings," said Don Sandefur, who met TP in 1973. "The IAAM, at one point was very restrictive in that you had to be a member to go into the business meetings and to attend certain events."

Hey TP, Come on In

But that didn't stop TP. "One of the first meetings I was attending, Tom walked right in with all the managers. I remember several people stopping him telling him that he wasn't allowed in," Sandefur relates. At that point, the person heading up the meeting told the crowd: "Look this is Tom Powell of *Amusement Business*, anybody have a problem with him being in here." Nobody said a word and from then on he was allowed in, paving the way for other AB reporters as well. TP sees it as a vote of confidence of not only his reputation, but that of the publication as well.

"TP is a success today because he made everybody feel like they were his friend and that they could confide in him," Sandefur said. "He was always fair and he never took a rumor and ran with it. In truth it's nearly impossible to do it all the time, but he does. He just won't do it any other way."

But being honest and fair didn't mean his personality and fun-loving spirit didn't blossom during those early days. At the IAAM convention in San Francisco in 1977, TP attended what he considered to be the most opulent party he had ever attended. It was hosted by the new owner of Holiday of Ice, Arthur Wirtz who also owned the Chicago Black Hawks NHL hockey team. TP and Washington D.C. building manager Jim Dalrymple decided they should go backstage and set up a picture of some Follies-type, scantily clad dancers. Having failed to get official permission to go back stage, Dalrymple knocked on the door, assured them that the two were from *The New York Times* and wanted to get a few pictures. "I shot pictures until I was too tired to shoot anymore," TP recalls.

VISITING THE BOONIES

"I ran the Rushmore Plaza Civic Center in South Dakota and invited Tom to our IAAM district meeting that we were hosting. Tom came in to cover the meetings and the first thing he said to me when I picked him up at the airport was that he had made more touchdowns than Red Grange on the flight to get here."

- Dick Geyer

Suite Times

One of the highlights of the IAAM convention each year was the AB suite, open each night with free booze, snacks, camaraderie, card games and a lot of story telling. It served as a fun haven for attendees who were tired of the trade show floor and client dinners.

Howard Lander, then AB publisher, remembers the first AB suite at the IAAM convention in Miami in 1981. "Tom and I made the mistake of staying in the suite. So about 4 a.m. Tom and I and several others were still up drinking. I felt that I was just about finished for the night. Tom was in the bathroom and I figured that when he came back I was going to go to the bathroom and not come back again. Well, it was Tom who didn't come back. He went to his room to bed and I was stuck in there entertaining these guys until 4 in the morning," Lander remembers.

The suites, from year to year were not only fun, but they were important for AB to sponsor as the newspaper was building its name in the facility industry. The suites made all the difference at that time. People who visited and stayed for one drink or for the night, would talk about the suite for months. It was the perfect situation in which to build the ever-important network of relationships.

Milton Rodgers, then manager of the Mid-South Fair in Memphis recalls seeing TP in the suites, all night long, night after night, year after year. "He was the spiritual leader of AB's hospitality suite that was clear."

SHHH!

In 1983, at TP's 21st IAAM convention, back in San Diego where it all started for him in 1972, and 11 years after the first AB suite was presented, Marriott Hotel officials did something no hotel had ever done before, it closed the suite down due to excessive noise. "We had been warned several times, but that wasn't new, just about every year we were warned about the noise, and had no problem," TP said.

Here, however, around 1:30 a.m., a security force of eight men entered the room, and told everyone they would have to leave. However, they offered an alternative room on the first floor where they could make all the noise they wanted. Everyone packed up and went to that room for several more hours.

37

THE TOM POWELL MEMORIAL SOFTBALL GAME

A few weeks prior to the Montreal IAAM convention in 1984, the idea surfaced to start up an annual softball game. TP would coach and play on one team with the other to be coached by Earl Duryea, then with Ringling Bros. and Barnum & Bailey Circus.

Don Sandefur played in that first game and remembers it quite well. "We had no gloves, and we all played barehanded with an oversized softball, which I called the pumpkin ball. Thaxter Trafton got a bus and arranged for a park. A couple of the concession companies came up with beer and we went out to the park with the main purpose of drinking as much beer as we played softball," Sandefur noted.

Nearly 60 people showed up for that first game, some to play, most to watch, all to drink. After 10 innings of play, AB publisher Howard Lander discovered that the beer had run out and immediately called a halt to the contest. AB's team won that historic game, 15-13. That set the precedent for the coming years. Whoever was ahead when the beer ran out won the game.

In the following years, the softball games grew more sophisticated and a lot more popular. It was Earl Duryea who started calling it the Tom Powell Memorial Softball game. They played on for 18 years and eventually moved from sandlots to major league stadiums.

Everyone Wanted To Play For TP

TP said in the early games there would be 12 or 15 guys to a side and Duryea would load up his team with the good players. Everybody wanted to play on TP's team because he made sure everybody got to play and that everybody got to bat. TP says the big difference between him and Duryea is that Duryea played to win.

"It was blood with him and he'd have bare bones, 10 people. I'd have women. I'd have old. I had Don Myers when he was 80-something years old playing with us and I made sure he got up to bat. Any woman could come out and I'd let her play with us," Coach Powell remembers.

The softball games were fodder for TP's columns for weeks prior to and for weeks following the games. No reader of AB could honestly claim he didn't know the outcome of that year's game and who played on each of the teams.

You're Out Of Here!

Bob Reid, now retired from Vee Corp. was a professional umpire for nearly 30 years on the high school and college level in Minnesota. He was the natural choice to be umpire for the softball games. Of course Reid received pressure from the two managers. "Earl would put more pressure on me than Tom because it was more important for Earl to win. He seemed to want to win more than Tom." Ray Ward was always the scorekeeper.

Earl didn't play, but Tom enjoyed pitching. "It was slow pitch where you lobbed the ball high. That kind of pitching is very hard to call strikes or balls," Reid said. But I didn't get too excited about it because I wasn't being paid." Was TP a good pitcher? "In slow pitch softball it's pretty hard not to be a good pitcher," Reid said.

One building manager who always wanted to play was Dick Geyer, but he was particular who he played for. "I never wanted to play on Earl's team. I wanted to play on Tom's team and he would let me play but he would always make me sit on the bench in the beginning and then put me in when everything was going to hell. That way he could blame me if his team lost," Geyer said.

> **DRINK TO THAT!**
>
> *"I was sitting in a bar one night with Tom and a stranger sitting close by was obviously watching and listening to us. Impressed with our conversation, he came over and said Tom has such a great mind that it should be donated to science when he dies. Another guy at the bar, overhearing that comment, turned around and said to hell with the brain, I'd like to have his liver."*
>
> *- John Hobbs, Nashville Palace owner*

On the other hand, AB's Ray Pilszak never played on TP's team. "I was always there for the games, but I made sure I wasn't on TP's team. I knew he would never win because he didn't take it that serious, so I was on the other team because I liked to whip his ass."

In addition to the competition and the drinking, the next best thing to these games were the venues in which they were played. During the years, the teams played in five major league ballparks. "The managers of those parks were great to us," Pilszak said. "They would have the big scoreboards running and they would really take care of us. It was really neat being on those fields playing where the big guys play and looking up and seeing us on the scoreboard."

TP, the coach and pitcher for the AB IAAM softball team.

Pilszak points out that the ballgames were just one example of how AB stayed involved in the industries it covered. "It was a uniqueness, a camaraderie that we had then, that I think we're missing today."

Too Many People

The interest and popularity of the games increased substantially when they started playing on the big fields and instead of 20 or 30, hundreds of people would come out and want to play. Some years they had to divide into four teams and it got out of hand. Everybody wanted to play and it was virtually impossible to get everybody in the game when you've got that many.

Harold Bannon, then assistant director of the Hartford (CT.) Civic Center had played in most of the games and was a bit concerned that the "originals" were being benched more frequently so the newcomers could play. He wrote to TP, partially with tongue in cheek, noting his and the other's loyalty to AB. "While we may be slowing down a bit, we can still drink with the best of them, which I believe makes us still a valuable asset to AB."

In spring 1997, TP announced in his column that he was retiring from the softball team but would continue to coach, which he did for four more years. TP didn't make it to the 2001 convention, the first one he missed since 1972, but he put Ray Pilszak in charge of the AB team.

In 2001, perennial opposition Coach Duryea, asked Frank Poe, then

IAAM president for a formal IAAM blessing for that year's game, set to be played in the L.A. Coliseum. The game had never been a sanctioned event of the convention and Duryea thought it was about time for official recognition.

Poe Calls It a Classic

Poe responded to Duryea's request. "I am not in a position to officially sanction a contest of such epic proportions. The Tom Powell Memorial Softball Classic has become a tradition so huge that a presidential decree could not alter, deter, or in any manner interfere with this contest. Therefore let this communication represent our acknowledgement of this non official event."

TP said the games got to be too big, and logistically, they got to be a hassle, lost most of their initial charm, and the last game was played in 2002. The following year AB dropped its public facility coverage and quit attending the IAAM convention.

The suite, the softball games, and the basketball games all helped *Amusement Business* acquire and keep a strong, positive reputation in the facility management industry. TP was amazed at how many thank you phone calls and letters he and the others at the publication would receive after a convention.

One such letter came from Michael Kelly, who was facility manager at the University of British Columbia in Vancouver. "Just a quick note to thank you for the continued support of IAAM. The AB hospitality suite is about the second most important activity at the conference. The softball game, of course, is number one."

38

TP GETS ROASTED

The IAAM regulars grew restless for something new in 1995. Even with the popular AB suite, the Tom Powell Memorial Softball Game and the myriad other activities at the IAAM convention still going strong, the gathering needed a shot in the arm, according to Don Sandefur.

"Several of us felt some special occasion might lighten the convention up a bit and add some excitement to it. We came up with the idea of having a special evening, a kind of a mix between a roast and a tribute to Tom," said Sandefur.

The Tom Powell Appreciation Dinner was held in the ballroom of the Colorado Convention Center in Denver on July 30, 1995. More than 350 paid $75 each to attend. By evening's end Tom not only had some pretty cool memories, but also a lot of loot, including several sports jerseys, a sports jacket, a gallon of Scotch and a check for what was left over after all the bills were paid.

TP rode into the ballroom on the back of a golf cart, as George Smith drove. He was supposed to make his entrance standing up in the back of the cart holding onto a special harness that was added to the cart earlier in the day. However, someone came by, saw the harness, knew it wasn't normally supposed to be on the cart and inadvertently dismantled it. When TP, along with Jim Dalrymple and Smith showed up to prepare for the entrance there was no time to rig another harness. It was decided that TP should sit.

The lights of the ballroom dimmed, the ominous "Spracht Zarathustra," the movie theme to "2001: A Space Odyssey" began playing as Christine was escorted to her seat on the dais. Once she was seated, the spotlights focused on the door, "Gonna Fly Now," the theme from the movie "Rocky" began, and in came TP on the golf cart. People stood and cheered, but TP doesn't remember being able to see anyone. The spotlight was on him and he couldn't see a thing. Smith kept telling him to smile and wave to the right.

Gary Lane, who was then head of the public facilities in Denver presented TP with a proclamation from the mayor proclaiming July 30, 1995 "Tom Powell Day" in the Mile High city.

Bad Jokes, Great Fun

While it was a great success in gathering TP's closest friends and admirers together, the evening was a creative bust when it came to humor. "I have never heard so many stupid, unfunny jokes and remarks from such a distinguished group in my life," remembers Tom.

Sandefur agrees and said it only got worse as the three-hour event dragged on and the presenters had more opportunity to drink. "That was the world's longest roast and as the evening went on, people kept leaving my table. I wound up sitting by myself. I said something to Tom afterward that I didn't know his life was so filled that it took all this time to mention everything," said Bob Reid.

Since that evening, Reid has found out more intimately about TP's long, action-filled life. Reid interviewed him for an oral history project. "I went to Nashville and we sat down in his office and we talked and talked for more than four hours." Not surprisingly, it was the longest of the 20-some oral histories Reid has taped for the Society for the Preservation of Professional Touring Entertainment History at the University of Texas, Austin.

"I'll tell you something," Sandefur said. "We asked everyone to limit themselves to two minutes and I don't think anyone did. Most just kept right on rambling, no matter what kind of signs and prompts I gave them. Next time I'm going to get one of those long poles with a crook at the end."

Among the attempts at humor that night, Earl Duryea noted that the liver of TP was the only one rejected by Mickey Mantle. There were a few groans and mostly silence. The crowd didn't get the joke.

Bill Waldo, of Country Roads, was mildly funny with his memories of going to dinner in Nashville at the Nashville Palace and "having a strange feeling" all evening. "After dinner I leaned back, stretched a little and looked up and oh my God, there was a picture of TP painted on the ceiling tile directly over my head. I then knew what caused that feeling during dinner."

Waldo added the final punch to the true story by adding that it "seemed natural for Tom to be hanging around in the bar." The ceiling picture is still there, among other bar regulars.

Bill Luther, a long time cohort of TP's noted during his two minutes at the microphone, that the "best quotes I ever used for myself came directly from TP's column."

AB's Lander & Pilszak Save The Day

Among the many bombs there were a few funny stories and funny presenters who stood out from the rest. AB's Howard Lander and Ray Pilszak approached the dais as a team and proved to be the most original of the lot.

Lander pointed out that through the years Tom had done some very offbeat and funny things. He called them TPisms. Pilszak's jokes and digs were among the funniest because they were true stories, like the time he went along when TP to help him buy a new car. It was a light blue Ford and he liked it as soon as he saw it, and said he would buy it.

"I kept saying to him. Tom, how can you buy a car without ever driving it. TP said he wanted the car and he bought it," Lander recalls. "About a week later he took it back complaining that the steering was stiff and it was hard for him to turn the wheel." The salesman then informed him that it did not have power steering. TP tried to get them to take it back but they wouldn't because it had been driven for a week.

Lander remembered the time that TP invited him, Pilszak and then AB sales manager John McCartney over for dinner, but before they could sit down to eat, they had to assemble the new dining room chairs TP had just purchased. He might not be mechanically inclined, but he definitely knew how to use his other skills, namely sweet persuasion, to get things done.

A few of the roasters at the Tom Powell Appreciation Dinner in 1995. From left are Don Sandefur, Paul Buck, Earl Duryea, TP, John Hobbs, Neal Gunn, Donna Dowless, and Bill Luther.

39

TP'S HEALTH ISSUES: WHAT'S UP DOC?

TP has never taken good care of his health. He has always eaten too much of the wrong food and has been overweight most of his adult life. He drinks too much Scotch, he pushes himself too hard to meet deadlines and with all the partying he does, it appears he never gives his body enough rest. Considering all this, it's amazing his first major health issue didn't occur until he was 50 years old, on August 5, 1983.

He was scheduled to drive to St. Louis with his friend Don Tatum to watch his beloved Philadelphia Phillies play the St. Louis Cardinals. "I didn't feel well, but I felt like if I could have burped I would have been okay. Not thinking it was anything big, I decided to make the trip anyway. When we got to our room in St. Louis, Gerry Baron who ran Busch Stadium had a case of beer waiting for us and I couldn't drink any."

They went to the game and had front row seats. In the third inning things began to fall apart. "I just threw up all over everything and everybody. "Gerry took me to the First Aid room and I got all cleaned up and went back and watched two more games. I wanted to see the Phillies and Cardinals. I couldn't eat or drink while I was there, not even a hotdog."

The next day he felt better and was the same old TP, eating all the wrong foods as usual. They drove home and remembering how bad he had felt decided to go to his doctor for a check up. The doctor sent him directly to the hospital. "He says you've had a heart attack, and as luck would have it the Phillies and Cardinals were on TV that night, Monday night baseball, the last game of the series and he wouldn't let me watch it because he thought I'd get too excited. I said, no, I promise I won't get excited but he wouldn't let me watch it."

TP Meets Dr. Fruits & Nuts

His regular doctor brought in a specialist who tried to talk reality with Tom. "I called him Dr. Fruits & Nuts because that's all he wanted me to eat. He looked at me and he said I was disgusting.

"He said you're a doctor's dream. He says you know how long you're going to live if you don't change your ways, and I thought he was going to say next week, and he said 12 years and I thought to my self, hell, that's not so bad."

TP doesn't know why he didn't go under the knife at that time. The doctor said "we'll treat it with medicine and exercise." As those 12 years started closing in TP started to think about exercising. He lost 30 pounds in six weeks. "I took his advice seriously for a while and watched what I ate and exercised, and then I went back to all my old habits."

Walking was TP's exercise of choice and he would occasionally go out at lunch and walk around the Music Row area, where AB's Nashville offices are located. "Every time I would get a good pace up, somebody would honk or would pull over to offer me a ride. Nobody was used to seeing me walk," TP said.

Singer Lee Greenwood pulled over and offered him a ride and didn't believe it when TP said he was out walking for exercise. Several booking agents, including Tandy Rice did the same. "It was nice of them, but it got to be a bother," TP laughed. "If my car had broken down and it was raining, nobody would have stopped."

Hip, Hip

Not wanting to miss out on the annual late winter and early spring fair and carnival conventions, parties, and especially the Super Bowl were major considerations when TP tried to come up with a date in late 1993 for a hip replacement. The doctors originally had the operation set for January 10, but TP got them to move it up to December 9 so he would have a "fighting chance" to attend some of his favorite activities.

During the approaching surgery, he spoke of it in his column and several readers contacted him, wished him luck and talked about their own hip surgeries. It turned out that he missed quite a bit, including the Super Bowl for the first time since 1981, and his gig as an after dinner speaker at the New Hampshire Fairs Association annual convention.

He had the operation on his second hip three years later on March 19, 1996. Again, he strategically booked the date with the doctors to make sure it fell after his favorite holiday, St. Patrick's Day. In his April 8, 1996 column, TP wrote that he had "almost forgotten" all the discomfort associated with hip replacement surgery. He said the main problem is that the recuperative period requires a great deal of patience, something that "I have never had much of."

While still in the hospital for that second hip surgery, he started receiving the first of hundreds of cards, fruit baskets and flower arrangements. John Hobbs brought TP a beer bottle with flowers that he picked in a local park on the way to the hospital, and a fruit basket, with a bottle of Scotch hidden beneath the apples and pears.

Following that second hip replacement, he let it be known in his column that he wasn't drinking and that he was totally bored. The late Bill Chiesa, of MetraPark in Billings, Mont., invited TP to the Big Sky Country to recuperate from the surgery.

"Why not come to Montana where you can join the hordes of press and write some drivel about the Unibomber. We'll issue you a gun, give you a fast pickup and you can travel around the state at your leisure writing stories as fast as you feel comfortable. We have no speed limit in the state of Montana. I can't think of a better place to bring your wife for a couple of weeks. We'll meet you at the border with a suitable weapon." Tom declined the offer.

Bruce McKinney, then chairman/CEO of Hershey Entertainment & Resort Company, sent a heavy box to TP at the office that was in turn taken to his home while he was recovering. Inside was a huge package of virtually every kind of Hershey candy product made. An attached note read:

"Understand a number of your friends have showered you with various and sundry get-well gifts. None, however, can or will match the therapeutic benefits of Hershey's chocolates. Thus to aid the recuperative process and put you back on the road to good health and continued happiness, I highly prescribe the enclosed filled prescription for chocolate."

What TP considers the funniest of the get-well gifts came from his friend, country music singer Pat Garrett of Strausstown, Pa. who also owns a sheepskin products shop. He sent TP a sheepskin rug with a note saying, "Anyone who's gonna be sittin' on his butt while healin', ought to have something soft to sit on. Try this."

The Sounds Of Pounds Dropping Off

Through the years, TP has seriously tried, and failed to lose weight on many occasions. His doctors finally gave up on scare tactics. Nothing worked, at least for long. In his column, TP would talk of the bets he made with other well-rounded industry figures on who could lose the most weight within a given period. He usually chose Lent as the time period and would usually lose a few pounds, only to put them back on quickly.

Knowing that alcohol consumption connotes weight gain, TP also gave up drinking for various periods and kept his readers abreast of the results. Again, he was successful for short periods of time. In 1986, he passed on a trip to Germany's famed Oktoberfest because he was "not imbibing" at the time and that the "lure of the massive beer halls" would be too much. "I just can't do it," he admitted.

The only time he was in "really good shape," TP says, were the two years he was in the Army when he weighed 175 pounds. "I was 134 pounds, much too skinny when I graduated from high school." He was "much too heavy," at about 280 pounds in 1992, when he told his readers that he had finally decided to do something about the weight.

Although it didn't last long, TP joined his buddy John Hobbs for an exercise class at Nashville's Vanderbilt Hospital. He talked about his first morning in his column. "Hobbs picked me up at eight this morning. He was in his glory as he told the physicians who supervise the exercise program that he had promised he would recruit somebody who was in worse shape than himself. Now he had delivered."

He wrote in his column that he partook in what is commonly referred to as a workout, something that he had managed to refrain from for most of his life, "like a parish priest shuns pagan rituals."

The Big C Scare

In late 2001, 18 years after his heart attack, and six more years than Dr. Fruits & Nuts had given him to live; TP was diagnosed with colon cancer. It was found early. "I had never had a colonoscopy and during my routine health checkup, the doctor said I should have one." The colonoscopy showed a growth, which turned out to be malignant, and surgery was scheduled immediately.

"After the operation we sweated it out while we waited for two days for Susan Briley, our doctor, to call. She didn't call by five when she was supposed to and we kept trying to call her. She called at 5:12 and we were scared and nervous, but she said the best words I ever heard: "no residual cancer," TP recalls. "That was a very happy, emotional day for the both of us," said his wife Christine. "We were both screaming and crying."

Don Sandefur was one of the first to talk with TP following that surgery. He said it was very clear that TP was scared. "I was talking to him a couple days after his surgery. Fear was in his voice and he was crying. It scared the hell out of him. There's no question about it. I'd never really seen him that emotional before. Never," Sandefur said.

While the heart attack concerned him nearly two decades earlier, the cancer scared him. However neither eventually served as his wakeup to living a healthier lifestyle.

"The cancer scared me because I think most people with it are goners. I lost my mother at 53 who suffered terribly, my first wife suffered terribly at 48, my brother suffered terribly and he was five years younger than me. People are still suffering terribly from cancer and I think it's inexcusable. I'm bitter about cancer."

Based on those past bad experiences, TP thought it was the end of the line when he was diagnosed with cancer. "I truly thought I was a goner. I mean how many people do you hear about that caught it in time or that they're going to be okay. I just figured this was it."

Several years later, TP wrote in his column that he had another complete physical, that it cost $60 and that he got a clean bill of health. "No doctor, not even a friend, will give a physical for $60," wrote Denzil Skinner, then head of Facility Management Group. "No doubt that is why you got a clean bill of health, the doctor only partly checked you out!"

TP has never been tempted to follow one of those fad diets. "I'm one of those guys who believes what he wants to when it comes to such subjects as smoking, drinking, what kinds of food are healthy, jogging, etc.," TP wrote in his column in 1995 following many years of people telling him how he should live more healthy. What he wrote appears to be a subtle way of getting back to everyone who kept telling him what he should do and what he should eat to get in better health.

"I figure that sooner or later a study is going to be done that says exactly what I want to hear. For instance, I'm of the opinion that in the very near future, the American Medical Association is going to release a study saying it's good to drink 19 or 20 Scotches a night, eat all the fried food you want, and smoke until you can't breathe. They're going to report that all the wrong foods which I eat now are what everybody should be eating."

GOODBYE FRIENDS

"Several of Tom's friends died within a short period a couple of years ago and that seemed to take a toll on him; it really bugged him for awhile. He said he was tired of writing Final Curtains (what AB calls obituaries) for his friends, but felt he should be the one writing them because he wanted to do his friends justice. There were so many friends dying so fast it was kind of scary. Who is next? I mean you can't help but think that. Will I be next?"

- Christine Powell

Living Life Out Loud

People are amazed at how Tom keeps right on ticking. He obviously abuses his body, he's overweight, in his older years his hips have kept him from exercising and of course there is his drinking. But something keeps him going.

Howard Lander thinks he knows why. "I think it's how he looks at life which is probably why he keeps beating the odds. When he had that heart attack a number of years ago, they were shocked that he got out of there. I think he doesn't have a lot of stress. He never worries about things. Maybe now he does but he never did then. He always enjoyed life and I think that's really what added to his longevity."

As editor, TP's management style never caused much stress for himself or his staff. If one of his reporters started stressing, he would walk over and calmly tell them that "everything will be fine. There's nothing that we can't handle."

Lander says Tom looks at glasses half full. He looks for the best in situations and the best in people. He has that boisterous laughter and he has a million great stories.

TP has an indomitable spirit, Wayne McCary thinks. "He's an example of a man who loves life, loves what he does, loves people and he loves the business. That's what fires him up everyday. His work is his life and his life is his work and that's important to him. He never complains either. I've never heard him belabor his illnesses or anything else."

Paul Serff thinks TP should serve as a "role model for all of us in terms of how to live life. Tom lives life out loud with full vigor and that's probably the way we all should. Not that we should all follow his bad habits, but we should spend a lot more time living and having a positive attitude. Tom lives the spirit of the industry."

Why Am I Still Here?

"Why am I still here when I have lost so many of my friends?," TP questions. " John Hobbs and I talk about this all the time. He's 75. We were both members of the Knights of Columbus. Just about everybody's dead but him and me. And I'm sure a lot of them lived better lifestyles than we do. I don't know. I don't question things like that. I'm just greatful."

It's obvious to all that TP certainly appreciates life. Christine sees TP enjoying life to its fullest. "I don't know if he could appreciate it more than he does." Tom and Christine live by a slogan: "Every day is Christmas Day and every night is New Year's Eve."

Christine adopted her current positive attitude when she and Tom got together. "It's hard not to, he's so positive, so gracious for every minute of every day."

The gang at Showtown Bar in Gibsonton, Fla., signed this special get-well poster following TP's heart attack. Bill "The Brush" Browning, the famous show painter created the poster.

40

TP INTERVIEWS PT BARNUM

In mid-1983, Ray Pilszak and TP were driving through New England, when they came across a large monument and statue of P.T. Barnum in Bridgeport, Conn.

"Hey, we need to stop and I'll take pictures while you interview Barnum for your column," the aging sales director told the editor. TP's entire column of July 23 was dedicated to that encounter with the "sucker born every minute" legend. It was full of humor and a lot of history about the greatest showman to ever live. It was one of the classic TP columns.

TP and PT.

"I wasn't always a winner," Barnum confided to TP. "Though I did hit it big, you might say, with Jumbo, an African elephant I purchased from the London Zoo and brought to the U.S. in 1882. Geez, that was over a hundred years ago and that word, Jumbo, is still synonymous with bigness."

Continuing Barnum said, "I tried to convince everybody that a genuine white elephant named Tokung Taloung was not a fake. For some reason nobody bought it and the term white elephant is still used to describe a business failure."

The temperature was about 95 degrees as TP stood there asking questions of a granite statue. Pilszak, who had been listening to the interview, asked TP if he would like a beer. That's when Barnum nearly exploded, according to TP.

"After all, Barnum had also been a member of the Connecticut Legislature and had been a famous lecturer on temperance during his 1810-1891 lifetime. I'll take a Coke, I told Ray. After all, I wasn't about to take anything for 'granite' in this weird interview."

41

AB STAFF ROASTS TP

In honor of TP's 50th birthday, on July 18, 1983, the staff of AB, headed up by Publisher Howard Lander, surprised Tom with a column that ran in the July 23 issue.

Titled "AB on TP," the heading of the column resembled a typical "TP on AB" column, but where Tom's mug shot usually was placed, there was a small group picture of the AB staff. In retrospect, the "roasting" that staffers did in this column was way funnier than those offered during the official TP roast 12 years later during the IAAM convention.

Lander abstained from contributing to the column citing that the man (TP) already has enough problems. "He's unloved, unwanted, slow of feet, dull of senses, has trouble communicating, lack of confidence and is void of any marketable talent. It would be wrong to hold such a man up to public ridicule."

Among the staff comments:

Steve Rogers, executive editor: "Never have I met anyone with such an incredible lack of a sense of direction. I witnessed Tom lose Atlanta while standing on Peachtree Street. Never have I met a grown man who needed so much help in dressing himself. I hide at conventions requiring formal attire. I was on my back three days after trying to stretch a cummerbund around him."

Cindy Acuff, production manager: "Tom's page layouts resemble a roadmap through a nuclear battle zone. His hand writing is like Egyptian hieroglyphics to our make-up people at the printing plant. That's how mistakes happen on our pages."

Len Durham, office manager: "When Howard said to be nice to you, that eliminated anything I could say about you."

Jim Helmer, sales: "(When TP entered the carnival world), little did Father Mac know he would be stuck with a self-appointed assistant chaplain who drank all-day and snored all night. The editorial staff knows they have to dress him on the many occasions he has to wear a tuxedo."

Ray Pilszak, sales director: "For years he led people to believe he was much younger, even claiming that he's still like a baby. That's probably true, since he never lost all of his baby fat. It's been preserved by all of that Scotch. He may be big, he may be humble, he may be aging, but he is one of a kind (the world couldn't handle two) and he's still our guy."

Pauline Gerson, sales: (In prose) - "From Mobile we thought we'd never get out; but after three tries we found our route. I learned that when you stop to seek directions; I'd better be listening - you pay no attention."

42

CARNIVALS: THE LONG LOVE AFFAIR

Working for a survey road crew during the summer of 1952, while attending the University of Scranton, TP was making $115 a week, more than he ever imagined he could earn.

A wallet-draining experience at a local carnival however, leaves one to wonder today how he grew up to be one of the staunchest boosters of the carnival industry.

He saw a shiny watch at what obviously was a flat store, a crooked game, and went for it and before he knew it, he had dropped more than $115 without ever getting the watch. "It's the same old story and it happened back then much more than it does now, but now I know that very few operators out there today condone that kind of activity," he said.

The carnival industry holds a place special in TP's heart. He met his wife Christine while she was a concessionaire and it's this genre, from the ride jockeys to the grease monkeys to the top dog, that probably know and love TP the most. He defends the carnival industry as passionately as he defends his friends. In one, he is the unofficial spokesperson for the industry, an ombudsman, and a fan.

Bob Johnson, president of the Outdoor Amusement Business Association (OABA) says TP is a valuable asset to the carnival industry. "Tom is the Bob Hope of our industry. A better ambassador we have never had. He's a generous contributor of his time to help those in the business and through all of his toastmaster work, he has brought laughs and a sense of family to show club members across the country."

The Times Are Changing

Back in the early days, TP laments, the carnival industry was more about characters and showmanship. Nowadays it's more like big business. However, the carnival business is still full of colorful characters. Through the years, TP has encountered such characters as Oklahoma Red Gates, John The Peddler Curtis, Benny the Bomb Koske, Popcorn Danny Craig, Burl

Camel Rider Nordine, Walk Away Frank, Louisville Junior and Louisville's son, Louisville Junior Junior.

One of TP's earliest and longest relationships with a carnival owner was with Rod Link, who passed away in November 1993. Tom's wife Christine had a food trailer on Link's midway and TP would visit often, and would work in the joint while going about his AB duties.

One day at the State Fair of Oklahoma, Link and TP noticed some "suspicious-looking" characters hanging around the midway and TP, putting on his reporter's hat, said he would investigate to see if he could find who they were.

They lied to him saying they were "just locals." Several days later, on one of the busiest days of the fair, with nearly 100,000 people on the grounds, their true identity was revealed. They were part of an Internal Revenue Service task force. They were part of a raid on the midway. TP picks up the story from there, a story that shows that above and beyond, the man stays true to both the industry and his friends.

"They brought trucks onto the midway and really endangered the safety of all the people out there. At the urging of Rod, I started antagonizing the force of 21 men and their commander by taking pictures, trying to show where they were damaging equipment and almost hitting people as they moved it. Look Rod, I would say. They scratched this and put a dent here. They started to really get ticked off and tried to get me out of the way.

"I informed them that I was doing my job, the same as they were doing their jobs, and I wasn't about to move. I walked right up to one guy who seemed to be the biggest jerk in the bunch and took his picture. Then I asked him his name, which I needed like a hole in the head. He refused to give it to me, playing right into our hands.

"I marched (I could do that in those days) to where the command post was set up, went to the top man and told him he had an agent who refused to give me his name. The boss walked back and asked me to point out the culprit, which I did, with glee. This guy, I said, pointing right in his face and the agent was informed to cooperate with me in any way I wanted.

"That night as I was counting change in Christine's joint, Rod walked by with what I thought was a big glass of water, and handed it to me. 'Here, you earned this, but I'm going to bed and I don't want you to bother me,' he said with a laugh. I almost gagged when I took my first sip. The glass was full of straight Scotch, I wasn't expecting that."

FEEL GOOD GUY

"It feels good just being around Tom. He emits a sense that he is really happy to see you. He has a great story for every occasion, and his extensive industry knowledge, ability to rattle off statistics, keen wit, and his love and enthusiasm for his work are utterly amazing."

- Franklin Shearer, Hersheypark

The Hot Sauce Caper

On one visit to see Jim Murphy of the Mighty Bluegrass Shows at the Tennessee State Fair in Nashville, TP and Murphy started talking about food and restaurants. Murphy asked TP if he liked hot and spicy foods and TP answered that he liked nearly all food.

Murphy likes to call this the hot sauce caper. "I gave him a spoonful of Insanity Sauce, supposedly the hottest sauce in the world," Murphy said. "TP took it and started having problems breathing and he couldn't talk because it was so hot. Once we got some milk into him, things cooled down and we started laughing, but he said he would get even with me."

That get-even day came nearly six months later during the Gibsonton carnival trade show. "I got to the club around 10 a.m. and couldn't find any parking spaces. There was only one spot available, the one reserved for TP. I figured it was early enough that he wouldn't be around for a couple hours because I knew he was out partying the night before."

Murphy parked in the spot and sure enough, TP showed up at 10:15, and realizing it was Murphy's car, had it towed. Murphy recalls that "TP found me later and said, 'now we're even.'"

Gibtown, An Amazing Place

The official gathering of the carnival and circus gang and those on the supply side who sell to them, gather on the grounds of the International Independent Showmen's Association (IISA) Club in Gibsonton, Fla. each February for the annual Trade Show & Extravaganza.

Today, most just call it the Gibtown Club, and the trade show itself is usually referred to simply as Gibtown. TP refers to the event as "the darndest convention you'll ever see," and "the most fun" of all the events AB covers. There are acres of rides, novelties, tickets, food items, lighting, and plush toys. Anyone with something to sell to the outdoor amusement industry is there peddling their wares.

The outdoor area surrounding the Gibtown Club is used as community ball fields when the trade show is not set up. Inside the club, a bar, dance floor, and meeting rooms are open during the off-season when the carnies, who make up the better part of the population of the community, are back in town from a long season of traveling.

The entire town is zoned as Residential Show Business, in the interest of carnival and circus people. Not only are Ferris wheels in your driveway accepted, they are almost expected.

Circus performers have high wires in their back yard, ride owners have their Tilt-A-Whirls and Scramblers set up on their front lawns getting them ready for the upcoming season. Food trailers and colorfully painted trucks are parked everywhere.

Throughout town you'll see the front line workers, the performers and the owners mingling together. You'll see the bearded lady, the 700-pound fat man, and the lobster family. Nobody looks at them twice. They're just part of the community and are members of the club.

> ## TP THE MENTOR
>
> *"I consider Tom both my good friend and mentor after working for and with him at AB for 10 years. We were so much alike in both our love of sports and carnivals and our physical stature. I heard comments all the time from industry people wondering if I was going to be 'the next Tom Powell,' and eventually replace him as the official voice of carnival folks at AB. To me, that was the ultimate form of flattery and I took pride that others thought enough of my work to mention me in the same breath as Tom."*
>
> *-Don Muret*

TP's Home Away From Home

The highlight of the Gibtown Club to TP is the bar. During the trade show, the bar is open from 10 a.m. to 3 a.m. and it's packed most of the time five deep. The drinks are cheap and everyone knows everyone else.

Father Mac, the carny priest said Sunday Mass at the club for many years, only a few yards away from the bar. But it didn't bother him, nor did it bother the drinkers. He often would join them after Mass.

Tom feels at home in Gibtown. The clubhouse is his castle and he is definitely the king of jackpots while there. For those not familiar with midway speech, jackpots is defined as "stories, often exaggerated," told between traveling showmen.

The auxiliary bar in use during the trade show is known as Coconuts. It's directly adjacent to the indoor trade show floor, across from the AB booth and is always packed. Tom has been given a personalized bar stool by IISA officials, and it is well used during the 6-day trade show. He shows up in the morning, makes a few rounds of the trade show and settles onto his stool, where he holds court for most of the day.

Everyone knows where to find TP. They come by with handshakes, pats on the back, and plenty of stories of their latest adventures. TP invites them to sit down, he pulls out his notepad and presto, another carnival story has been put in notes, to be written at a later time. He walks away from the club each night with more stories and more photos than the rest of the reporters combined. Maybe more importantly, he walks away with a fresh supply of inside information about the industry.

He doesn't have far to walk to his car, he has also been presented with a reserved and personalized parking space, the closest to the club anyone is allowed to park during the trade show.

Charlie Knows Where To Find Him

Charlie Cox, owner of Concessions by Cox, has been in the business for nearly 50 years and not only runs a multi-state concessions and a special events company, but also manages and promotes fairs and festivals. He knows his way around. And he knows TP.

"I learned a long time ago that if I'm at a meeting or at a convention and need to make contact with TP, I don't call his room or go to the AB booth, I go to the bar. If he is in attendance, that's where he'll be," Cox said. "He'll be sitting there talking, drinking and more often than not, he'll have his camera and hid notepad right there on top of the bar in easy reach."

The affable Cox who is quite a legend in his own right, says he is in awe of TP's ability to mingle with the entire fairgrounds crowd. "He talks with everyone, from the ride operator to the games agents to the fair manager to the carnival owner," Cox said. "And it's not an act. He truly and sincerely loves this business and all the people in it. That's what I think is really neat."

Cox said he is also in awe of TP's durability. "That guy just doesn't slow down. He's always out there with his people, learning more about what's going on in the industry and who's doing what with whom. He doesn't gossip and most of the time you don't even realize you're being interviewed. He just talks with you as a friend and I'm sure he could really tell you some great, revealing stories. That could be another whole book," Cox laughed.

Showing His Friends Around

In 1989, the two top officials of the International Association of Amusement Parks & Attractions, visited Gibtown for the first time, and TP was there to help acclimate the two. Dennis Speigel of International Theme Park Services was president of the parks group then and John Graff was executive director.

"What can I expect to see?" queried Speigel. TP smiled, pointed out a few things and started introducing the two to a few carnival owners. "They went off on their own and less than an hour later I saw them and they said they felt right at home," TP recalls. "The two industries have a lot in common, especially the people."

The most popular year-round watering hole in Gibsonton is the Show Town Bar, originally owned by Andy and Ethel Osak and now operated by their son Chuck. Andy and TP were friends for years and one day Andy said he wanted to do something special for the people at AB.

He says "I'd like to set up a Polish picnic" and he put out this nice spread of cheese and polish sausages. It's now been going on for more than 20 years. Bill Alter always comes, Father Mac and Father John Vakulskas Jr. usually show up, as does Albert and Dennis Carollo from the Iron Mine attraction in Michigan and Nick and Lorrie Ludes from National Ticket Company are usually there.

Dick and Barbara Knoebel started coming during the early 1990s and Dick always brings along a soupie, which is a huge hit with not only the invited guests but the rest of the bar as well. Somewhat on the order of pepperoni, they are flat links of air and salt cured pork sausage. Knoebel goes into the kitchen and slices up the sopresatas into thin little pieces, and everybody loves them. He adds: "They are perfect for a picnic and they wash well with beer."

TP was immortalized on the front of Show Town Bar for years until Foster Maples drove through the front of the building destroying the painting of TP that famous carnival painter Bill "The Brush" Browning had painted nearly a decade before.

As one of the most prolific single copy salesmen of *Amusement Business*, Andy had the painting of TP and a copy of AB done to promote the fact he sold the paper in the bar.

> ### JACKPOTTING
>
> *"Tom will talk with friends for hours, but he doesn't like negative talk or gossip. He'll tell me to quit gossiping when I'm hanging around our friends in Gibtown, but I'm not really gossiping. We're just talking carny talk and not really gossiping, but I am more careful what I say when I'm with Tom."*
>
> *- Christine Powell*

Man Of The Year

When carnival owner Jimmy Drew became president of the Miami Showmen's Club in 1997, it was his duty to pick a man of the year. "My first choice was TP but I figured he had already been chosen before," Drew said. "Since he was the only person I really wanted, I researched and found that he hadn't been chosen before. I got him!"

Ad in Amusement Business honoring TP as Man of the Year for the Miami Showmen's Association.

MIAMI SHOWMEN'S ASSOCIATION

TOM POWELL
1997-1998
MAN
OF THE
YEAR

Florida's First Showmen's Association is honoring Tom Powell as the 1997-1998 Golden 100 "MAN OF THE YEAR." Tom Powell (TP) has been an avid supporter and friend to the Carnival Industry for more than 25 years. Since 1972, Tom has worked as reporter, editor and now Associate Publisher of Amusement Business news weekly. His dedication to and coverage of carnivals has kept communications open and available. He has sat on the dais and served as emcee at many Showmen's Club banquets throughout the years.

A contribution to this year's plaque will show your appreciation for Tom and support of the Miami Showmen's Association.

Super Block: $5,000 • Giant Block: $2,000
Double Block: $1,000 • Block: $500
Single Name or Title: $100

As a contributor, your name will be inscribed on the plaque which will be hung in the Club's Showroom.
Mail your check to:
Miami Showmen's Association
3391 Griffin Road, Fort Lauderdale, FL 33312
Pledges may be made by phone:
954-967-0073 or Fax 954-962-9234

John Campi
Project Chairman

James H. Drew III
Club President 97-98

43

TP CLIMBS ONTO HIS SOAPBOX

While quite opinionated in his own right, TP seldom took the opportunity to bare all, to share his deepest convictions with his readers. However, sometimes he felt he had to speak out and when he did, he used his column as his official soapbox.

He grew up in a coal mining and railroad town where unions were necessary for the good of the working class and he has always been a union supporter. But he has challenged the union on several occasions on its worth in professional sports.

Being an avid baseball fan for all his life, Tom put it on the line in 1985 when Major League Baseball went on strike. Most of his August 17 column was devoted to the strike, a labor action that he called incomprehensible. The action itself upset him, but when he started hearing interviews with some of the players who he had followed and respected for years, he went even further into madness.

He wrote of the player's high salaries, their great playing conditions, and the lucrative pension plans. He talked with former ballplayers and stadium managers who also couldn't understand the strike action.

Those Damn Ball Players

"I say let 'em go, forever. Damn those ball players. What am I going to watch on TV?" In a half-apology for his ranting, he told his readers. "Right now, I'd like to assert that I'm glad I have the opportunity to say what I feel in this space. I'm happy I can come to work every day to a job I love!

TP on TP

"I always vote straight Democratic ticket. I always told my kids I'd forgive them for anything except voting Republican. Ironically, my dad was the only Republican and Protestant in our neighborhood. When I first voted, I voted Republican because my father was paid something like $25 to deliver five votes. You can bet mine was one of them."

- Tom Powell

In October 1987 when the National Football League went on strike, he spoke out again. "Nobody making more than $200,000 a year needs a John L. Lewis or a Jimmy Hoffa to argue his case," TP wrote, noting once again that unions have no place in sports. "If anybody needs a union in sports, it's probably the front office people and the officials, who in most cases are grossly underpaid."

He goes on to say everyone, including himself feels they are worth more than they are paid and that companies who risk their money in business, deserve to keep the lion's share of the profits, assuming of course they pay fair wages. The players "think they should share in every extra dollar of revenue that accrues to owners." He points out that "unfortunately in the past" owners have "buckled in to the absurd demands."

He goes on: "It's inconceivable that athletes would ever strike, but they're doing it and I hope the owners hold out until hell freezes over." The following week, he read where the Newspaper Guild might back the football players by not attending scab football games and by lending financial aid.

"I've heard it all now," wrote TP. "Some guy probably making less than $1,000 a week is being asked to aid guys making a million dollars a year. I still don't believe the union is asking its members to do that, it's ridiculous."

It's Rock & Roll And He Likes It

When Tipper Gore started speaking out on rock music censorship in 1985, TP responded quickly. Tom and Al Gore were both reporters at one time for Nashville's daily newspaper, *The Tennessean*, and TP is a ticket-voting Democrat, but Tipper's attempts at censorship were just too much for him to take.

"Like religion, I happen to think that choosing what song to listen to or what television program to watch are personal things that should be enforced at home." He then went a bit further criticizing Tipper. "As Frank Zappa, of whom I'm definitely not a fan, said, angry housewives shouldn't try to force their views on the masses."

In June 1980, TP dedicated his entire column to a personal, heartfelt message about a movie he had just seen, "Carny." He had high hopes for a great show when he first heard about the motion picture, but upon seeing it, he was greatly disturbed. "If anybody thought carnies were the scum of the earth before witnessing this move, their beliefs have not been shattered. As a matter of fact, that crummy, creepy image of carnival people is fortified by this movie.

"The carnival people of the movie are bums, freaks, perverts, toughs and crooked politicians. Nobody denies this has been a part of carnival life, but never the dominating force, or even a good percentage of it."

He went on to challenge the industry leaders, by name, to not sit back and remain quiet. He asked for letters from individuals, from association leaders. He queried. "I wonder if show owners around the country will comment on this movie or simply sit back and let the barbs continue."

In subsequent weeks, the letters poured in and most were printed in AB's Letters column or in TP's column. The most vociferous response came swiftly in a phone call from Herb Israel, a concessionaire and manufacturer. After saying he "nearly threw up" when he saw the movie, he proposed that the Outdoor Amusement Business Association get behind him in a $50 million class action suite against the movie's producers. That suit was never filed.

TP The Liberal Democrat

Politics normally didn't get TP's dander up, but religion often did. "Lawlessness and the influence of criminal elements are subjects being tossed around by Nashville preachers who are hoping to keep pari-mutuel wagering out of Tennessee," he wrote, noting that he hopes everyone votes for the wagering come election day.

He then reminisced that when he arrived in Tennessee's capital city Nashville in 1958, the serving of alcohol by the drink was illegal and that "preachers and bootleggers did their best to keep it that way for a long time. I thought that was about as hypocritical as you could get."

Following a long dissertation on the silliness of the entire situation, he wrote, "Why can't preachers give sermons on sin and going to heaven or hell, instead of trying to legislate morals?"

TP started off his July 15, 1989 column with a simple statement: "For what it's worth, I think Pete Rose is guilty as sin. However, I also think he should still be admitted to baseball's Hall of Fame." He noted that if he were to be found guilty of betting on his own team, he would "unfortunately receive a lifelong suspension" that would keep him out of the Hall of Fame.

"I believe that he must be responsible for his own behavior, but his remarkable accomplishments as a player should not be overshadowed by his shabby, seemingly out of control gambling behavior."

Closing his column one week in late 1991, TP came out of the blue with this rhetorical question. "I just thought I'd ask why Pete Rose went to jail for gambling and Magic Johnson is being eulogized for contracting HIV, the AIDS virus. Did I miss something?"

You Ain't Nothing But a Hound Dog

Regarding the television coverage of the late Elvis Presley's 58th birthday in 1993, TP was miffed at how negative the media portrayed Col. Tom Parker, the man who created the Elvis legend. "You can say or think what you want, but if not for that old carny from Holland, Elvis could have been another Tommy Edwards or Fabian, rather than the King he became."

He went on to say that Parker's methods may have been unorthodox, but they worked and when the "audience left it was wanting and craving more." TP pointed out that Parker certainly controlled Elvis, but the other entertainers of the time who weren't controlled tightly, usually ended up as "flash in the pan" acts.

The late Parker was an active member of the Showmen's League of America right up to his death and he seldom missed a meeting of the SLA in Las Vegas.

During the summer of 1993, TP climbed onto his soapbox again when officials of minor league baseball implemented a ban against the use of tobacco products by players, managers, coaches and umpires at minor league baseball parks. The hypocrisy continues, he wrote. "It is an egregious mistake to impose this law and even worse to enforce it. For the record, I feel the same about the use of seat belts."

Let's Go Ride The Big Bass

Gaylord Entertainment officials announced that its popular Nashville theme park, Opryland USA would close at the end of 1997 to make way for a huge mall and a Bass Pro Shop retail outlet. The news didn't rest well with TP.

"The sad part is Opryland could and should be a great destination amusement park, doing as well as any," he wrote in October 1997. "I don't pretend to have the answers, but I don't think my grandkids are going to be begging mom and dad to take them to another retail outlet or the Bass Pro Shop."

The following spring, he lamented about the fact the city now had two professional sports teams but no theme park. "I hate to keep beating a dead horse, but I can't for the life of me figure out how Mayor Phil Bredesen (now Tennessee Governor) thinks the city will be better off with the Oilers (now Tennessee Titans) of the NFL, the Predators of the NHL and a MALL by replacing a carousel. Somebody's getting taken for a ride and it's going to be a costly one."

In 2000 when Opry Mills opened, TP scoffed at the local coverage and at the positioning efforts by Gaylord Entertainment officials by promising that "Opry Mills will be as much fun as Opryland was." TP noted. "My grandkids still want to go to Disneyland."

44

TP TRAVELS THE FAIRS CIRCUIT

TP is bullish on the concept of fairs and festivals.

"A lot of people are doomsayers saying fairs aren't going to be around for long, that they are outdated and hold little interest for the new generation," he says. While he admits that programming and activities at fairs will have to change with the times to stay fresh, he doesn't agree they are doomed.

"I say as long as there are kids there will be fairs and carnivals. It's just like in the arena business. The Harlem Globe Trotters; I've seen them a hundred times and could care less if I ever saw them again but every time you go you see little kids laughing and going nuts, and that's why they're still around because there's always more kids coming. And kids will always want to ride rides and do all the things that are associated with a carnival or fair."

During his career at AB, TP has visited more than 100 different fairgrounds and has gotten to know the top fair officials at the largest U.S. and German events. He has visited the cow barns, the pig barns, and the top executive's offices. He has eaten the food and has seen some great musical concerts in the grandstands. He loves fairs and still enjoys the environment they create.

On The Fairgrounds

From a concessionaires point, one commodity that is often hard to get on the fairgrounds is drinking water. Most concessionaires use bottled water or have supplies of water brought in. TP was a victim of a water shortage at the LaPorte (Ind.) County Fair. Concessionaire Stan Minker was there.

"There was a bar on the fairgrounds and as we all know, Tom drinks Scotch and water. One hot day he was having a few cocktails at the bar. I was there, but not sitting with him. The bartender came over to me and said 'You know that guy from the AB? I don't mind all the Scotch but it's hard getting the damn water. I wish he wouldn't drink so much water in his drinks.'" Minker recalls, laughing.

Tom made his first visit to the Eastern States Exposition in West Springfield, Mass. in 1981, and Chief Executive Wayne McCary wanted to do something special for him. "We sent a limousine to the airport to surprise him. We had told him we'd provide him with wheels, but we never said anything about a chauffeur."

As TP got off the plane, he saw a man in uniform holding up a sign with TOM POWELL on it. At that point in his career, TP wasn't yet use to the limo life. "The driver insisted on not only carrying my suitcase but my camera bag as well," TP recalls. In the back, there was fresh candy and chilled champagne. "Mark the driver insisted on calling me Mr. Powell and said he would continue to do so, even over my objections."

"We consider that a touch of class," the driver told TP. "And don't open any doors. You'll only make me look bad." That set a dangerous precedent McCary laughs.

Returning To The Big E

When Tom and Christine returned to the Big E in 1996, one of the first people they met on the fairgrounds was McCary's 82-year old mother, Bessie. When she found out who TP was, she told him a story about when McCary was 11 years old, the only present he requested for his birthday was a subscription to *Amusement Business*, which was then known as *The Billboard*.

"I had a tough time getting her to pay for it, too," said McCary. "I had been getting copies and hiding them under my bed. When she saw that the paper contained routes for carnivals, circuses and fairs, she was afraid I was going to run away with the circus."

McCary used to enjoy walking the fair with TP but realized that he didn't have time to do it every day. "Going through the fairgrounds with Tom Powell is the equivalent of going to a campaign stop with Bill Clinton. You need a hell of a lot of time to get from point A to point B because he wants to stop and talk with everyone, no matter who they are, and as you know, there is never a two minute conversation when you talk with TP."

George Smith, who managed a building in Des Moines, Iowa, experienced the same thing when TP visited the Iowa State Fair and asked Smith to come along with him to the fair. "He borrowed a golf cart from Jim Murphy, whose Mighty Blue Grass Show was playing the midway. He didn't want to drive it, so I did. I called it the Tommobile," Smith remembers.

"I drove him around like he was the Pope. He waved to the people, and he knew everybody. He'd go by the big concessionaires, the small concessionaires and they all yelled to him. He was like a king on the midway. Before he and Christine got serious, he knew all of the very nice-looking, available women out there and that was one of his trademarks."

Early Fair Treks

In 1980 on his first trip to Richmond for the State Fair of Virginia, he received another royal ride from the airport to the fairgrounds. A big green, antique Packard convertible

> **KNOWS HIS PEOPLE**
>
> *"No matter where you are, TP will know somebody."*
> - Tony Conway, Buddy Lee Attractions

was waiting for him. The car, as it turns out, had been used to haul luminaries around Virginia on special occasions. A sign was attached to the car welcoming him.

In his column reminiscing about the journey, TP wrote "I now know how government officials feel as I waved to shouting youngsters and oldsters who surely wondered who the heck Tom Powell was." During the drive to the fairgrounds, one of the signs on the car blew off, came into the car and slammed against TP's head. However, all was well when fair manager Cork Teachworth met him at the fairgrounds and whisked him off quickly to the grandstand where Jim Sorgi of American Fireworks set off a display that lighted the sky with "WELCOME TOM POWELL."

While inaccuracy is never good, especially in a newspaper, a typo in AB in 1980 caused a few smiles. In an article about the Indiana State Fair accepting midway bids for a two-year run, AB inadvertently printed that the contract would be good for the 1881-1982 seasons. One astute reader wrote in. "A contract for 102 years would be very, very nice." TP answered with "I think most midway operators would agree."

Thanks to a press trip organized by Kathy Gangwisch, a publicist for the Jim Halsey Company, TP attended his first Neewollah (Halloween spelled backward) Festival in Independence, Mo., in 1980. The annual Halloween festival brings in big carnivals and big name talent.

During that visit, he mingled backstage with the likes of Roy Clark, Roy Orbison, The Oak Ridge Boys, Merle Haggard, Ronnie Milsap and Don Williams. He also met his first Russian, Anatoly Dyuzhev, the cultural attaché of the USSR Embassy in Washington D.C. Dyuzhev presented Tom with a copy of "Soviet Life" with an inscription that read "To my new friend, Mr. Tom Powell."

Too Many Fairs, Too Little Time

In addition to visiting the fairs themselves, TP and the rest of the AB staff is busy each year, usually during January and February traveling to meetings for the various state and regional fair associations.

The late Bill Chiesa, who first served as manager of the Montana State Fair then the MontanaFair, sent an invitation to TP for the Rocky Mountain Association of Fairs meeting in Great Falls, Montana in 1982. It was one of many invitations he received for various state meetings that year.

Chiesa put his tongue in his cheek and wrote this classic to TP: "I continue to read of your extremely busy schedule and how tired you are. On behalf of the Rocky Mountain Association of Fairs, which will hold its annual convention here in Great Falls, hosted by the state fair, I would like to invite you to a meeting where you can come and rest.

"Tom, there is nothing to do here in Great Falls, so obviously, the only thing you could do is rest. No large crowds, no nightlife, no theatre, no baseball stadiums or large covered domes. Remember, its too cold to play golf, hunting season will be over, and all the rich girls you would want to meet would probably be in Phoenix or somewhere in the South. So why not be the first-ever editor of *Amusement Business* to cover our annual convention?"

It worked! TP printed the letter in his column with his reply. "Okay Bill, please consider this as my acceptance. How can I resist such an alluring invitation."

OK Bill, I'll Be There

Several months later, TP arrived in Great Falls to one of the most memorable "and shocking" welcomes he ever received. "As I attempted to drag my suitcase and hanging bag into my room, I looked up and saw a beautiful, scantily-clad girl sitting on what appeared to be a bona-fide hospital bed," he recalls.

She greeted him, asked him if he were Tom Powell and when he confirmed, she handed him a bottle of Chivas Regal Scotch. "She then sidled up to me just as the door burst open and in came Chiesa with a photographer and a host of other people trailing behind." The girl was dressed in a Red Cross outfit and they had brought in the bed as a gag.

The next morning when Tom was delivering an address to the 412 members present, Chiesa introduced him by telling the crowd what happened. When TP went up to the microphone, he acted tired and winded. "Sorry, I'm out of breath, but that girl came back again last night." The crowd roared with approval.

Chiesa also sent creative missives to TP each year trying to get him to visit the fair. However, he wasn't as lucky on those invitations. The last invitation TP received for the fair before Chiesa died in 2002, was sent in late August 1999. It read, in part: "I'm not really sure how much longer I'm gonna be here, and as I look at the pictures of you, I'm not sure how much longer you're gonna be there, so if we're going to do this Tom, it's about time you get here."

Myles Johnson, then manager of the Clay County Fair, Spencer, Iowa, also made an elaborate plea to TP to visit his fair. In fall 1988, Johnson wrote and pasted color pictures on a note that ran 55 inches in length. It read: "In past years we have attempted to lure you to our fair. To date, all invitations have been declined. We have tried to entice you with a list of things to show you what makes our fair unique, but that didn't seem to work."

In the past, "We have tried to entice you with the offer of a beautiful, sleek limousine, complete with a nattily-dressed chauffeur." A picture of Johnson standing next to a tractor was pasted next to that one.

"We have tried to entice you with king-sized drinks," with a bottle of Jack Daniels pasted adjacent; "and we have tried to entice you with thin girls (with a photo of six beautiful slim women with few clothes on) and fat girls (another very large photo), but to no avail." Johnson closed the note by attaching two suggested mini-tours of other fairs in his area that TP could take in at the same time, along with talent lineups and dates for each.

It didn't work that time either, but TP started his column the following week by noting that he had received phone calls from "13 women in 12 states and nine letters from eight more states" wondering how Myles obtained copies of their pictures.

Visiting the Big E, from left, OABA President Bob Johnson, Big E President Wayne McCary, TP, and petting zoo owner Bob Commerford.

45

THE LAS VEGAS GATHERING

Fair officials and showmen from around the country gather the first week of December each year in Las Vegas for the International Association of Fairs & Expositions trade show and conference.

Taking place concurrently with the fair convention are separate meetings and functions of the Outdoor Amusement Business Association and the Showmen's League of America. It's a huge week for the outdoor amusement industry.

In carnival and fair circles, "Vegas" is synonymous with these functions, just as "Gibtown" is synonymous with the carnival convention in Gibsonton, Fla.

Among the social events during the week is the popular Balloon Peddler's party. It's quite a party and Col. Blake Coleman, president of the group always makes sure Tom is invited. TP has the only reserved seat in the house for the event.

To demonstrate the attitude of the party, here's how the invitation reads: "From 4 p.m. Till Dead Drunk. Police officers will be in attendance, and as drunk as the rest. And the bouncer is the first one sober. There will be no search for drugs, weapons or contraband. Celebrities include millionaires, sports figures, bums, beggars, stars, gutter merchants, bootleggers, horse players, crap shooters and countless others."

Don Sandefur remembers his first trip to the Vegas convention. He was there with TP. "My experience with Tom was always through IAAM because I've been part of that organization for more than 30 years, first as a building manager. So, when I first went to Vegas with him and we walked through the hotel lobby and he would call everybody by first name, I was impressed."

At the 1981 Vegas gathering, TP met Art Linkletter who claimed he loved fairs, most significantly, the Arizona State Fair. However, his reasoning for loving it was for a totally different reason than most of the others in attendance. Linkletter recalled that 18 years prior, he had played the Arizona State Fair and stayed at a dude ranch nearby and was transported to and from the fair each day by helicopter.

Linkletter explains the rest: "Each day as I flew in I'd spot pieces of land that I wanted to buy. I wound up buying several parcels and making millions of dollars from the deals. Yes, I have fond memories of that fair."

Dennis Speigel, president of the International Theme Park Services in Cincinnati, Ohio, was president of the International Association of Amusement Parks & Attractions in 1989 and he attended the IAFE that year representing the parks group. Speigel knew few of the regular crowd in Vegas. However, he did know TP.

> **THE LAST OF THE COWBOYS**
>
> *"TP is certainly one of a kind and in a way I think he's the last of his kind. The industries are changing, the newspaper is changing, and everyone's expectations seem to be changing."*
> — Charlie Cox, concessionaire

"Tom offered to take me around and introduce me to some of carnival people, a group I had never been around much. We hit all the great parties and the first person we met was Oklahoma Red, and the first thing Tom did was ask him how he was doing. 'Pretty good Tom. Ain't got no new tattoos and haven't been thrown in jail, so I'm doing fine.'

"Then Tom said, 'Come over here Dennis, let me introduce you to someone I haven't seen in a while, Alligator Annie.' She was quite a fun lady, especially when she pulled down her top and showed me her nipple rings. I believe that was the first nipple piercing I ever saw," Speigel said. "Tom certainly knows some cool people."

The hottest scoop TP could find in Vegas in 1988 concerned the whereabouts of Elvis Presley. It came from Col. Tom Parker, Presley's manager. Looking TP straight in the eye, the always jovial Parker responded to the question concerning the stories that Elvis had been seen alive in Kalamazoo, Mich.

"Everybody thinks they know what is going on, but I know exactly where Elvis is," Parker told TP without hesitation and without a joke in his voice. "He's at Graceland in Memphis, Tenn. He's buried there."

46

THE TRAVAILS OF DR. TOM

TP claims the odds of getting sleep during the conventions in Las Vegas are slimmer than the odds at the tables in the casinos.

One year, following a hectic late night of partying on the final night of the activities, TP overslept and missed his scheduled flight to Nashville. He rushed to the airport hoping to get another morning flight, but was told nothing was available and that he would have to wait and possibly be able to fly out on standby later that day.

While sitting in the airport coffee shop waiting, carnival owner E. James Strates showed up and the two ended up in deep conversation for nearly two hours. "We were so engrossed in talking, I forgot to leave my ticket with an agent to put me on standby for the next flight out. It was going to Dallas and I would have been able to connect to Nashville from there."

Before long, a group of others, with valid flight reservations to Dallas, started showing up and sat down with TP and Strates. Showmen Billy Baxter and Bill Dillard were there, as was Buddy Lee of Nashville-based Buddy Lee Attractions. TP said he had forgotten to take his ticket up and Dillard said he would do it. He walked up, put the ticket on top of the pile and told the agent that "(TP) is my personal physician and I can't travel without him. There must be some mix-up for him not to have been assigned a seat by now."

Buddy Lee, the last to arrive, got into the gaff and asked loudly if "Dr. Tom had been assigned a seat yet." Dillard then moaned a little, slumped toward his wife, Helen, and said in view of the airline agent. "I'm not feeling well. I don't think I can go on without Dr. Tom."

Dillard was informed, in no uncertain terms by the completely unsympathetic airline employee that "If you don't feel well, sir, you had better not get on the plane."

The con had failed, but in true TP fashion, things turned out for the best. It looked dismal at first. As the plane loaded and TP saw that he was the last of 50-some other standby flyers, he didn't think he had much chance to get on that Dallas flight.

It got down to two seats and the agent called for a specific party of two.

One person walked up and said he was flying by himself and only needed one seat. The agent looked at Tom and handed him the last boarding pass for that flight.

Only one seat remained and TP was seated in First Class, a few rows in front of the Dillards. Seeing him arrive, the Dillards smiled, and asked the flight attendant for a double brandy and said Dr. Tom had prescribed it for him.

"Feeling a little faint after all that tension, I prescribed a double Scotch for myself, too," recalls Dr. Tom.

Legendary sideshow operator Ward Hall and the legendary editor.

47

EPILOGUE: THE BEAT GOES ON

November, 2003:

TP turned 70 years old in July 2003 and he still has the passion for the travel and the curiosity to write those countless stories still untold by the myriad friends he has in the industry.

When asked if he would do it all over again TP quotes Spencer Tracy from the 1958 movie, "The Last Hurrah." "Yes, I'd do most of it all over again, but without the glitches."

What's in the near future for TP and Christine? "Everybody asks me why I don't retire. It's my life and I enjoy it. Even though I don't have the same role now as I did, I still love AB. I love the job. I love the people in all the industries and I would miss them."

The sign says it all, on the Powell farm in Starke, Fla.

Tom says he "was lucky enough" to be at the right age, 67, when the bill was passed in the late 1990s that allowed a person to earn all he wants and still collect full Social Security benefits. "I'm now getting a regular check from them. I feel like I want to work a while longer, earn my AB salary and get Social Security as well because I've been paying into it all my life."

For now, he says, he would like to keep working, but would like to work out a deal in the future that would let him spend more time working from the farm he and Christine own in Starke, Fla. Since the mid-1990s, he has used the farm as home base and has worked from there for several months each winter covering the many events held in Florida during that time of year.

The farm has a big sign out front proclaiming the property to be "Powell's Scranton South, Home of On The Earie, Established 1991." While TP and Christine live in the house, the farm's acreage is used by a local farmer to graze cattle. TP and Christine don't have anything to do with farming, nor do they intend to. "I get nowhere near the cows," he says.

"He may not live there full time yet, but he already is a celebrity in that little town," said concessionaire Bill Lordy. "The Big-O is his favorite watering hole and everyone knows him there."

Family Ties are Still Tight

Tom checks in with his four children "at least once every day," and talks with his four grandchildren, who call him Papaw, as much as possible.

He becomes a bit melancholy when he speaks of his children. "I can't begin to describe how proud I am of all four of my kids. I love them with all my heart. I have always wished I could do more for all of them to make life easier and without problems, which of course is impossible, but I try. The same is true with my grandkids," Tom says.

Julia, TP's oldest offspring has a Masters degree from the University of Virginia and a Doctorate from North Carolina, is a CPA, and lives in Yorktown, Pa. She is married to Paul Mulherin, whose parents once owned Yank's Diner in Scranton, where TP hung out in his teens. They have two children, Joseph and Rose.

Alice, the second oldest is a paralegal, lives in Nashville and has two sons, Chance and Casey. TP sees Alice's boys quite often and loves spending time with them. He'll often leave work early, pick them up from school and spend time with them in the afternoon.

His youngest son Kevin is an engineer and a graduate of Tennessee Technological University and lives in Nashville. His oldest son, Tommy, graduated from Middle Tennessee State University and has a master's degree from Vanderbilt University. He's a nurse practitioner in Dallas. Both boys remain single.

Tom continues to love Christmas and can become quite sentimental and nostalgic during the season each year. He plans to continue the

The Beat Goes On

Standing behind their proud papa are Alice, Julia, and Kevin. Seated next to TP is Tommy.

tradition of setting up his Lionel Train around the Christmas tree this year, the same train that has circled his tree every year since his first Christmas in 1933. It was a birth present from his uncle Marty Hutchinson. "It's a prized treasure and I look forward to it each year," he says.

They are Healthy & Happy

Since his bout with colon cancer in 2001, TP has had no serious health problems. He has slowed down his drinking while at home, but he still travels, works, and parties as hard as he ever has and he hasn't found an exercise program that he can stick with. Christine travels with him on nearly all his trips. She tends to him daily and when they travel by car, she drives while he reads the newspaper.

Would he be bored if he retired? "No way," said his wife Christine. "He would still have his friends, his family, and his baseball." Tom sees baseball as an important part of his future. There's an expression in the carnival business that goes "I love you honey but the season's over." It's about couples who get together for the season and then part their ways at the end. When baseball season starts TP tells Christine, "I love you honey, but the season has started."

He says as long as there is just one baseball game on television, he has something to do and he doesn't care who's playing. "I'd just as soon root against the Braves as I would cheer for the Phillies and the Red Sox. I'll watch any baseball game that's on television."

TP says he now prefers staying at home to going out. "I don't like to go to live events anymore. I've gone to a million in my life, but it's too much of a hassle now. By the time you park and you get in, I'd just as soon be at home watching them on television.

"My life will continue to revolve around sports whether I continue to work full time for AB or not. I always say if you can make it to opening day you've got to make it through the season to find out who won it all. I'm planning on being around at the end of the season. I want to see who wins."

Meet Tim O'Brien

As senior editor of *Amusement Business*, the world's number one business to business newspaper for the amusement park and attraction industries, veteran news reporter Tim O'Brien has learned to spot a good story when he sees one.

After working for and with Tom Powell for 18 years, Tim felt it was time to tell the world about the "real, larger-than-life celebrity journalist."

Tim's specialty areas of reportage at the newspaper are amusement parks, theme parks, waterparks, amusement rides, tourism, roadside attractions and tourist destinations.

Since joining *Amusement Business* in 1985, Tim has visited more than 500 amusement parks and has ridden more than 400 roller coasters in 17 different countries. He is a regular contributor to CNBC News and Travel Channel Radio, is quoted widely in the national press and is a sought-after guest for Travel Channel TV documentaries and news programs, thanks to his vast knowledge of the business side of amusement parks and roller coasters.

A graduate of The Ohio State University with a master's degree in journalism/film production, Tim is also an accomplished photographer and public speaker, having lectured extensively at industry seminars, local high schools, and various civic groups.

In 2001 he was presented the coveted Lifetime Service Award from the International Assn. of Amusement Parks & Attractions for his devotion and his "long-term achievements in the amusement industry." He was the first journalist to win that accolade in the association's 75 year history.

When he's not traveling, he's at home base in Nashville, Tennessee, where he lives with wife Kathleen, and his two daughters, Carrie and Molly.

Tim's published books include: "TP on AB, The Life & Times of Tom Powell," "The Amusement Park Guide," "Tennessee Off The Beaten Path," "Where the Animals Are," "Fun with the Family in Tennessee," and he penned "The Essential Guide to Six Flags Theme Parks" with his daughter, Carrie.

Enjoy all of Tim O'Brien's Books!

TP on AB: The Life & Times of Tom Powell. The illustrious story of the former editor and now associate publisher of Amusement Business trade newspaper. With 60 photos, the book introduces the reader to TP's colorful friends, his wife, former bosses and the many sports and music celebrities he has rubbed elbows with during his 30-plus years at AB. Relive his experiences through fun stories from both TP and his friends.

The Amusement Park Guide, Coast to Coast Thrills. The best selling and most complete guide to North American amusement and theme parks, waterparks, and family entertainment centers ever published. The colorful guide describes the parks, the rides, the activities and special events and provides driving directions. A history of the industry, various charts, and special sections on carousels and horse carvers, roller coasters, and dark rides are also included. Fifth edition; 325-pages.

Tennessee Off The Beaten Path. See the best of the fun and funky the Volunteer State has to offer! You'll travel gravel roads up and down mountains, through abandoned railroad tunnels, across the deltas and the plains. Visit fun and unusual fairs and festivals, quality folk art galleries and museums and discover the best places to eat and stay, from tasty meat and threes to fun bed and breakfasts. Sixth edition: 238 pages.

Give a Book to a Friend or Colleague

❏ **Yes!** I want ___ copies of the softcover edition of TP on AB for $18 each, which includes the book, shipping, handling and applicable taxes.

❏ **Yes!** I want ___ copies of the special edition hardcover copy of TP on AB, with a CD-ROM of TP telling stories, singing and talking about his larger-than-life career. Include $42 for each copy, which includes the book, CD, TP and the Author's autographs, First Class mailing, handling and applicable taxes.

❏ **Yes!** I want ___ copies of the latest Amusement Park Guide for $17 each, includes the book, shipping, handling and applicable taxes.

❏ **Yes!** I want ___ copies of Tennessee Off The Beaten Path for $15 each, includes the book, shipping, handling and applicable taxes.

To order, use the convenient order blank below or send a check or money order. To get your copies quicker, sign on to www.casaflamingo.com and use your credit card to make the purchase. Books are usually shipped within 48 hours.

Name _____

Company _____

Address _____

City/State/Zip _____

Phone _____

E-mail _____

Check our Web site or contact us for special quantity discounts, starting with as low as 10 books.

Make your check payable and send to:
Tim O'Brien • Casa Flamingo Literary Arts
6224 Deerbrook Drive • Nashville, Tennessee 37221
www.casaflamingo.com • tim@casaflamingo.com

Give a Book to a Friend or Colleague

❏ **Yes!** I want ___ copies of the softcover edition of TP on AB for $18 each, which includes the book, shipping, handling and applicable taxes.

❏ **Yes!** I want ___ copies of the special edition hardcover copy of TP on AB, with a CD-ROM of TP telling stories, singing and talking about his larger-than-life career. Include $42 for each copy, which includes the book, CD, TP and the Author's autographs, First Class mailing, handling and applicable taxes.

❏ **Yes!** I want ___ copies of the latest Amusement Park Guide for $17 each, includes the book, shipping, handling and applicable taxes.

❏ **Yes!** I want ___ copies of Tennessee Off The Beaten Path for $15 each, includes the book, shipping, handling and applicable taxes.

To order, use the convenient order blank below or send a check or money order. To get your copies quicker, sign on to www.casaflamingo.com and use your credit card to make the purchase. Books are usually shipped within 48 hours.

Name _____

Company _____

Address _____

City/State/Zip _____

Phone _____

E-mail _____

Check our Web site or contact us for special quantity discounts, starting with as low as 10 books.

Make your check payable and send to:
Tim O'Brien • Casa Flamingo Literary Arts
6224 Deerbrook Drive • Nashville, Tennessee 37221
www.casaflamingo.com • tim@casaflamingo.com

www.ingramcontent.com/pod-product-compliance
Lightning Source LLC
Chambersburg PA
CBHW051432290426
44109CB00016B/1526